To Bangladesh
And Back

Stephen Kellegher

PURPLE UNICORN MEDIA

Published by Purple Unicorn Media

ISBN 978-1-910718-07-0

PURPLE UNICORN MEDIA

INTRODUCTION

This book you are about to read is a day to day account of the things I did, the things I ate, but most of all the people I met when I went to Bangladesh for a holiday. It tells of when I was feeling fit as a fiddle to being sick as a dog. Also being brought to the brink of tears through happiness and sadness, to me it was like stepping back in time, none of the modern appliances like washing machines or things like that, the roads and the shops were not very modern either, no shelf stacking order whatsoever, if it fits it goes there, even the people seem to come from the past too. Many times during the holiday the things people would do or say would take me back to when I was younger with things like, going to the neighbours for your mum when you wanted your dinner or tea, nowadays many of the people won't even know the next door neighbour, all throughout the holiday I can only recall one or two fights which is not bad for a three month stay. The book also gives the weather and the places I stopped and the houses I visited, all in all I hope you, who are about to open it have as much fun reading it as I had living it and also I hope you get the chance to do what I did and it will be something you will always remember forever.

BANGLADESH

We have many natural advantages, our land is soft and fertile. So our borrowers can dig, plough and prepare the soil with their simple hand made tools. We can also cultivate most of our land. Many countries have big mountains, many countries have deserts and waters, so these countries do not have much cultivable land. Ours is again a tropical country so our soil gets enough sun, air and water, as a result we can easily grow better crops. The effect of our large population on our land is that there are one thousand people for each square kilometre, that is to say on an average each person has only 0. 1hectre of cultivable land, this amount of land is too small to produce just enough food for our existence.

Nahina Choudrey

DAY ONE   : Sunday 13 March 1994

LOCATION   : Penrith, Cumbria.

DESTINATION : Sylhet, Bangladesh.
TEAS :00

WEATHER   : Wet and windy

Well the first leg of the journey went okeh and we arrived in London around midnight after a six hour car journey from Cagney's Tandoori, the Bengali Restaurant in Penrith where me and Abu work. We got in to Abu's mum's house which was quite close to Upton Park, which is whoisit's ground erm, anyway I met and got introduced to Abu's mum, his elder bro and other relatives that were there to greet him, cousins, friends etc. I'm not saying there were a lot there but by the time he had said his hellos and that it was time for bed, so we were showed where we were sleeping said our goodnights and that and went to bed thinking only five more days in London and then the serious travelling begins, Oh by the way I knew West Ham played at Upton Park I was taking the piss.

GOODNIGHT AND GOD BLESS

DAY TWO   : Monday 14 March 1994

LOCATION   : London.

DESTINATION: Sylhet, Bangladesh.
TEAS :00

WEATHER   : Sunny and windy

Didn't do much today apart from meeting more mates of Abu, went and had a trip and seen a bit of London in the flesh so to speak which would be fantastic if there wasn't a trip to Bangladesh in the pipeline. then we went back to Abu's mums had something to eat watched a bit of telly and because I was in London the programmes were a bit different from up Cumbria, then hit the sack again now its only four more sleeps till my big adventure

GOODNIGHT AND GOD BLESS

DAY THREE   : Tuesday 15 March 1994

LOCATION   : London.   DESTINATION : Sylhet, Bangladesh.
TEAS : 00

WEATHER   : Raining with sunny intervals

Not much done again today but to be honest my mind is not in London only my body I'm to busy thinking about the trip of my lifetime have only been to Blackpool and the Isle of Man I'm not exactly your Christopher Colombus but we had a trip to Ilford and went to Valentines Park, but the weather put a stop to the walkabout so we made our back home to Plaistow in the east end because Abu needed his jabs, I've already had mine in Penrith and I have to take a course of malaria pills every day for a week before going and three weeks after I get back, so I got in touch with Carol Vorderman so she could work out how many of the fuckers I had to take with me and so I started taking them on the same day we set off from Penrith. After he had his jabs we went back home had a bit of tea watched a bit more cockney television before I hit the sack again still with the voyage of my life on my mind three days and counting.

GOODNIGHT AND GOD BLESS

DAY FOUR   : Wednesday 16 March 1994

LOCATION   : London.   DESTINATION : Sylhet, Bangladesh.
TEAS : 00

WEATHER   : Dry and windy

Been a bit more active today went to town to do a bit of shopping for bits and bats to take with us such as sun cream, insect repellent and last but not least stuff in case I get the shits which I guarantee I'll get which I would be able to handle having been on the piss a few times in my life its catching malaria I'm more worried about you don't get mozzies where I live so I don't know what the f* malaria is apart from its a disease that I've never had before and don't want to get later either. after the shops we went back to the house to drop our stuff off, have a bit of tea and get ready to go and have a game of snooker at the local hall, we had a few games and me and the guy I was partnering won and on the way home passed the Blind Beggar pub where one of the Krays shot George Cornell so today I've done a bit of shopping, taught Abu a lesson in snooker and seen a bit of gangland history but it still hasn't stop me thinking of what's happening in a few days I'm off to bed now.

GOODNIGHT AND GOD BLESS

DAY FIVE   : Thursday 17 March 1994

LOCATION   : London.   DESTINATION : Sylhet, Bangladesh.
TEAS : 00

WEATHER   : Sunny and windy

Started the day today meeting Abu's cousins and went to another park this one's called West Ham park and if I say so myself a very charming one at that. Then it was back home to get changed for this big traditional meal to sort of send us off on our merry way hosted by, let me get this right Abu's brothers wife sister who's name I've forgotten only for the fact that I've met so many people since I've been in London that my head is swimming with names and places in Bangladesh we should visit when we get there, I wouldn't mind were only going for three months, whatever her name was she did herself proud there was beef curry, chicken curry, fish curry, boiled rice, rice with beef in, you name it, it was on the table or if it wasn't on the table, it was in the kitchen because it wouldn't fit on the table, then after about two hours of non stop main courses all the desserts came out. next we had to go and visit Abu's mums brother but not before getting our passports, visas and tickets now I feel like I have one foot on the plane already and still a couple of days to go too. More food and tea at Abu's cousins then came home to go to bed been quite eventful tonight whether I will sleep tonight or tomorrow night for that matter who knows, better still who cares,

GOODNIGHT AND GOD BLESS.

Not a lot done today apart from a couple of games of snooker again and non other than Ronnie O'Sullivan was in playing a few frames with a friend of his and Abu let on "alright" but back in Penrith the way Abu went on about him you would have thought they went to school together, at least I'd a said alright Ronnie. after the games of snooker we did a bit of last minute shopping then it was back home to bed not long left now to the big flight 12 hours to be exact so its goodnight England for the last time for three months, GOODNIGHT AND GOD BLESS

DAY SEVEN   : Saturday 19 March 1994

LOCATION   : London.   DESTINATION : Sylhet, Bangladesh.
TEAS : 00

WEATHER   : Sunny.

I'm really excited this morning as you would expect, I've been looking forward to this trip for ages or seems like ages but it's finally here and do you know what, I haven't a clue what am supposed to be doing after I packed my last few things to take with me, so I just sat around while everybody else who knew what was going on did the business. After everything was sorted out it was time to go to the airport, the bags and luggage had already been put in the car the only things missing was, you guessed it me and Abu, so me and Abu got in the car and we set off for Heathrow Airport, after about a 55 minute drive and a whistle stop sight-seeing tour of London which was just the one attraction(if you can call it an attraction)the Houses of Parliament we arrived at Heathrow airport at around 12. 30pm to catch the flight which was due out of Heathrow at 2. 30pm. after all the rigmarole of saying goodbyes to Abu's family and the friends that had come to say their goodbyes and then there's the passport stamping, the frisking, and the checking of boarding passes and after all that finally me and Abu are on the plane, so now the trip is now a reality not some thing I've been imagining for the last few months. The plane took off and got into the air and I thought if that's lift off I didn't need the spare pair of underpants after all, just heard next stop is Paris to re-fuel, so lets hope I don't need the undies after the next take off gonna sign off now till we land in Paris.

LOCATION   : Paris, France

DESTINATION : Sylhet, Bangladesh.
TEAS : 00

WEATHER   : Raining

Arrived in Paris at 3. 15 GMT, 4. 15 cet, so in the air for the first time in my life for 45 mins, I haven't pissed or shit myself, I've not tried to open any doors or windows for a bit of fresh air and I haven't lost it, so I can safely say I will get to Bangladesh without incident. We were on board the plane waiting to re-fuel for about a hour and I must admit I was on, bored!, but I know the next stop when we get off I will be far from being bored. because the next stop is Dhaka Airport, in Bangladesh. I can't see anything exciting happening on the plane that going to take my mind off what I'm about to discover in a third world country I've never been to before, so now its around 9 0'clock GMT they've been round with the in-flight curries, so I'm going to try and get my head down for a few hours if I can before we land in Dhaka, so this is another first for me, trying to get to sleep at an altitude I can't count up to, flying above terra firma in what I can only describe as a Winston Churchill cigar tube with seats in, wish me luck. GOOD FLIGHT AND GOD BLESS, cos I doubt I'll get any sleep.

DAY EIGHT   : Sunday 20 March 1994

LOCATION   : Dhaka, Bangladesh

DESTINATION : Sylhet, Bangladesh.
TEAS : 00

WEATHER   : Sunny and Humid

We touched down in Dhaka airport and the flight was ok to me as I have never flown before and its been that long since Abu had flown so he didn't know whether it was a good or bad flight either, so we Arrived in Dhaka undecided about the flight at around 2pm GMT so that made the time in Bangladesh 8o'clock in the morning and it feels like its the middle of the day with the heat, when we got off the plane and got out of the building and we hit the Bangladeshi air I thought I was getting put in the oven the heat stopped you in your tracks, you didn't want to go any further in case it got any hotter, to make it worse we might have to wait 5 hours would you believe before we can get a connection flight to Sylhet, that's half the time it took us to get to here from England.

We did have to wait the 5 hours and it was boiling and I must have lost about 3 pints of sweat, when me and Abu got off the plane we looked quite smart, getting on the next one we looked like two piss heads coming out of the sea after having a swim fully clothed, the clothes we had on was literally stuck to us. We did manage to get something to eat at the airport in the 5 hours we were hanging around tho. when we did get on the plane it was 3pm in the afternoon Bangladeshi time and only took a hour and arrived in Sylhet at 4pm, we got through customs ok because Abu's two sisters, his uncle and a couple of friends were waiting, has I walked closer towards our entourage I began to realise I was the only white person in Sylhet airport and yet another first for me I was the ethnic minority. it was more trouble getting passed all the beggars outside the airport than getting passed the custom officers inside the airport, but when we finally did and we got into a couple of taxi's we made our way to Abu's sister's house in the middle of Sylhet sounding the horn each time we approached any kind of transport including people walking dicing with death dodging all the different kinds of vehicles, why, well according to Abu were VIP's that's why he honking his horn non stop. By now I've lost all track of time as I am to busy taking in all the brand new images my eyes are taking in, all the unhealthy smells my nose is handling, and all the different noises that my ears are trying to separately identify, it's a different world to what I'm used to. after what was to me a magical mystery tour we got to Abu's sisters Asma house and we got introduced to all the family and friends who had turned up at the house to welcome him back, I wont try and name them all or my holiday would be over so I'll introduce them as I write about them, while all the formalities were going on, the maid Shazia was making the tea and the rice for my first meal with the people I will be stopping with in Sylhet for the forth coming months. after the meal Abu's sisters Pharal and Asma unpacked the suitcases me and Abu had brought back, which had things like strawberry jam and stuff for all the kids, clothes, toys, and stuff for school, then we chatted a while, me trying to pick up words in the conversation I understood until we were shown where we were going to sleep for the holiday. so me and Abu got changed and went to bed so we can make an early start tomorrow with our big adventure, GOODNIGHT AND GOD BLESS.

DAY NINE   : Monday 21 March 1994

LOCATION   : Sylhet   DESTINATION : To see Sylhet
TEAS : 01

WEATHER   : Raining and sunny

Would you believe it, I was woken up this morning by of all things the rain, and I mean rain, that's the last thing I would have expected, later on in the year yea, but now no way, it was like the monsoon season come early. I've travelled over 5, 000 miles to be woken up by the rain, just my luck, I could have stopped in Penrith for that. Me and Abu had a bit of breakfast before we took the kids to school they had been given the morning off because Abu was here, met their teacher and I greeted him in Bengali which took him by surprise and when he told me to sit down in Bengali and I did, he was even more surprised. Abu spoke to the teacher for a bit before we came home, it wasn't that far to the school but because of the heat it felt miles away. We stopped at the house a while to chill out for a bit before we went to the shops to buy a few things for the hot weather such as a longee, which is basically a cotton tube the length of a skirt to wrap around your bollocks, a pair of flip-flops, I've not wore socks since I arrived and doesn't look like I will be either, so what a waste of space in my luggage eh!. after we got back from the shops Abu's sister Asma took me to the neighbours where they fed me cakes and tea and I spoke a few Bengali words and I was taught a few Bengali words, soon after we left and went back home to watch a bit of Bengali TV, they do have a TV set but it's only black and white, when I came the first thing I thought was I'd gone back in time, houses half built reminded me of old derelict houses half fallen down. some places no electric only lanterns, we were lucky we had electric, I say lucky but the lightning soon put a stop to that and our leccy went off too. so I ended up learning a few more words and phrases in Bengali with the kids before they went to bed, soon after they'd gone the lights came back on again, for half a hour then went off again something else that reminded me of times gone by, power cuts, then it came back on again only this time it was on 20 minutes and went off again, the next time it came on it stopped on until we'd gone to bed it was really weird seeing the lightning and not hearing any thunder like egg and chips without the egg, tomorrow were off to the village for the first time, I got enough looks when me and Abu took the kids to school and we didn't meet that many people on the way there. so tomorrow when there's gonna be about 2 or 3 hundred people buzzing around the place I can see my face getting worn out with everyone looking at it. so it's early to bed, early to rise makes a man healthy, wealthy and wise as my dad used to say and probably still does.

GOODNIGHT AND GOD BLESS

DAY TEN   : Tuesday 22 March 1994

LOCATION   : Sylhet   DESTINATION : Durgaphasha
TEAS : 04

WEATHER   : Sunny in Sylhet and it's sunny in Durgaphasha.

I am glad to say I wasn't woken up by the rain last night or in the middle of the night to be more precise, but I hardly got any more sleep than normal because of the heat, but am not complaining. It's 10am and have had me brekkie, a couple of chapatis and filling, a cup of tea and I've taken my pills, so I'm ready and raring to go down and hit Durgaphasha.

Only three of us went to the village, Abu's brother-in-law Anwar (who we call Bisab)Abu and me, we walked down the part of the road that wasn't fit to walk down let alone get a rickshaw or a vehicle up or down it. when we reached the tarmac where the town began Bisab started to try and hail a rickshaw by shouting O'DRIVER, followed by our destination, after a few went by one said something back to Bisab who swiftly replied by calling him an arsehole, a few more went past before we managed to get one after a bit of bartering of course, we were on the move, I must admit some of these lads or some of the older guys must be pretty fit to peddle people around all day, plus in this heat. When we arrived we got dropped off in the town centre and I've never seen such organised chaos in my life, Rickshaws, bicycles, motor-bikes, cars, buses, and lorries, big lorries all trying to get from one place to another in the quickest time possible, I tell you what a sight, I was just waiting for the carnage to happen before We got on the bus that must have past its MOT around the early 70's, brand new that in Bangladesh but it got us to Shunam Gong, after yet more bartering we got another rickshaw only this time we hired 2 one for Bisab, and one for me and Abu, after a shortish trip we arrived at the village I looked at it and thought "take me home "it was something out of the stone-age, no electric, no gas, no running water, straw roofs, not thatched just straw, but having said that it was the best day yet. Abu and Bisab went to see Abu's dad's grave in the next village and left me in our village for about a hour, I thought here we go a hour of twiddling my thumbs, wrong!, with my broken Bengali and all the villagers broken English, we got on like a house on fire and when Abu got back I was playing football with about 20 of the villagers age from 2 to a couple who were about my age, who says you can't enjoy yourself without a telly. after we had something to eat we came back home, travelling the same way as we got there rickshaw, bus rickshaw which dropped us at the edge of the tarmac before we had to get off and attempt to walk up the road without breaking a bone, twisting a ligament or just going arse over tit, after walking up the road like someone climbing Everest we arrived at the house around 8. 30pm and was taken to the neighbours on the other side for tea and cakes, then it was back home for a few more Bengali lessons until the lights went out so we called it a day. after about a hour and half the lights came back on again and we had supper which reminded me of something I forgot to write last night, Abu's older sister Pharul said with arm out stretched to Abu said Abu my brother, then stretched her arm in my direction and said you my brother, I could have been eating the most expensive food in the fanciest restaurant with the richest people in the world but it wouldn't have meant has much to me has it did when Pharul said it. well it's just started raining again so it's off with the lights and on with my longee, the good thing about this Bangladeshi rain it rains through the night,

GOODNIGHT AND GOD BLESS.

DAY ELEVEN   : Wednesday 23 March 1994

LOCATION   : Sylhet   DESTINATION : Around town
TEAS :05 and 06

WEATHER   : Sunny.

Went yet again to another house for tea that's the 5th one to press as you can see at the top of the page but I had to remember them all, until I started to draw little cups at the top of each page in my original diary. we were going to have another house visit but Abu and Baboor got left behind so Bisab and me had to wait because we thought they'd got lost, so he took me round town to look at the shops and that, and if you can't haggle or barter with the shopkeepers in Bangladesh then your gonna go home with what you come in, no set price or owt. how much 2 taka, al give you 1 taka, no!1 taka 50, done, shake hands and it yours. one easy lesson on shopping in Bangladesh. Me and Bisab arrived home at around 4. 30pm after walking round town for about a hour looking for Abu, Baboor and the family to turn up. In the house was Shazia, the cook and cleaner and Ishmael the water boy and the kids. while we were waiting for the rest to arrive me and the kids had a mad half hour before I had to have tea on my own as Abu and the rest of the family were longer than we had expected, when they did arrive back it wasn't long before I was whisked off again for another cup of tea in someone else's' house, bit of a chat, then back home where more chat was had until one of the girls Dilruba asked me if I watched the A Team cos it was on the telly, so I went and watched the A team on a black and white TV, which took me back a bit too, but out of all the episodes that were made I got to see the one with Boy George in whoopee!, but I was still glad to see a bit of telly tho. soon after we had watched the A team there was this thunderstorm, and I mean thunderstorm, not your normal hailstones that are the size of hundreds and thousands these were like malteasers, or ice cubes from heaven I called them, and them coming down on a corrugated tin roof that was what I called noise, even the kids screaming trying to talk to me and they were stood next to me, it was impossible to hear what they were saying, that's noisy. The ice cubes from heaven lasted about 10 minutes but the rest hung around for another hour at least, as soon as the hailstorm had finished everyone piled outside to see what the fuss was about, that's when we found out the size of the hailstones, more like pebbles. all the kids went collecting all the ice cubes from heaven in pans, so when it melted they had plenty of water, I never thought of that, being from Manchester if hailstones came down that size in Manny we would call it ammo to pelt the other kids with, so I was still deciding which team to join when they walked past me and took all the pans into the kitchen, although it was still raining it was quite warm so we all had a bit of fun for about 15 minutes with the old ice down the back of the neck trick, they even know it in Bangladesh. Then we all filtered back into the house to dry off and get ready for bed, so it's ON with me longee, OFF with the light and INTO bed so it's good night from me and a good night again in case you didn't hear me the first time GOODNIGHT AND GOD BLESS

DAY TWELVE   : Thursday 24 March 1994

LOCATION   : Sylhet   DESTINATION : At home
TEAS : 06

WEATHER   : Sunny

I like this Bangladeshi weather, it rains when your all in bed, and sunny when everyone is out and about. The trouble is I've not been out much today because I've got a upset stomach, which I expected, but I thought I might of lasted longer than 12 days, but I'd brought something with me for it and took some of that. Then I just dossed about the house all day in between going to the hole in the floor and a walk on the hills, passing these lads who were playing cricket and Abu told them I was Ian Botham, what's more laughable they believed him. wonder who else I've been, was wondering why everyone was calling me Clint, after the walk we came back to the house had a bit of food before a few more Bengali lessons and just having a good laugh in general, to say I had a bad belly today I have still had a good day. GOODNIGHT AND GOD BLESS

DAY THIRTEEN : Friday 25 March 1994

LOCATION : Sylhet DESTINATION : Nowhere!
TEAS : 06

WEATHER : Raining in the morn, sunny in the afternoon.

It was raining this morning when I got up, so after a bit of brekkie and I had taken my pill I ended up watching Spiderman and Tarzan with the kids, the only three English programmes on the telly and now I've seen them all, so if I don't want to go home with a few army deserters and start swinging from the trees and climbing the building I'd better have some more Bengali lessons, by the way the kids are not wagging it, they don't go to school Fridays, best not tell the kids back in England they'll be on a four day week. still raining but washed my shirt on the front door step, came out pretty clean too. then when the rain had eased a bit we went for a bit of fresh air and went for a walk on the hill for another staring session from the locals, them that haven't seen me before can look for a good five minutes, if it had been a good day I can sometimes attract a crowd, should get meself a cap so they can throw their takas in, rate I'm going it would pay off my holiday, even the staring session got cut short when two of Abu's cousins came looking for him, another staring session, but that soon stopped when I greeted them and asked their names in Bengali, Abu and I man took them back to the house for refreshments and we had a another chat and a cup of tea, (I would just like to say the tea's I can handle the chat sometimes gets a bit confusing) we went to the other room to plan the next day trying to fit in another invitation to one of Abu's cousins, that took enough time to have another cup of tea. Then no sooner had we done that more of Abu's relatives arrived at the house, at this rate I'll be talking fluent Bengali and have a "tea" belly by the time I do go home. More mayhem before supper, then after supper we all chatted for a while then all went to bed,

GOODNIGHT AND GOD BLESS

DAY FOURTEEN   : Saturday 26 March 1994

LOCATION   : Sylhet   DESTINATION : In the house
TEAS : 06

WEATHER   : Raining all day

Well it pissed down all day from about 2-15am when the rain on the roof woke me up, I thought awf. . . here we go again or words to that effect, the kids started screaming and then the people from next door who live in a shack, and I mean a shack, it was a mud hut to be kind, at least the house I'm staying in is made of breeze block, came banging on the door for shelter, as I looked to see what was happening the lightening struck and lit the house up and that's when I noticed the floor was at least 3inches under water, lied in bed I felt like a frog on a lilly pad, by this time everyone was out of bed, grown ups, the kids, Shazia and Ismael the help, and went into one room until the worst of it had gone, I wouldn't mind but its not even the monsoon season. After the storm everyone went back to bed. Picture it fork lightening, thunder that would shatter a decibel meter, monsoon rain and hurricane force wind, it was the worst storm I have ever been in "hellish" the light were on and off like Blackpool illuminations, the candles got blew out that many times I thought we were going to run out of matches and it was the coldest day to date, I'm saying that to me it was still warmish it's only because a couple of the women had jumpers on as well as the kids that I thought it must be cooler, when we got up this morning the floor was quite dry, considering, all the rain that covered it last night early morning whatever you want to call it, when the weather's like this all the days and nights roll into one big week. After breakfast and my pill me and Abu just dossed about the house all day looking at the damage the storm had done, the next door neighbour was next to homeless, the roof was gone the sides were flat but still there and the fixtures and fitting were probably in Dhaka. Tanvir spent about a hour and a half playing with a load of empty fag packets as building bricks, made me laugh you'd never get away with that in England. watched a bit more Bengali TV when the power was on, then me and Abu had a walk on the hill for a bit of fresh air in between showers and went back for tea, this weather is not very good for filling up my pages, when the weather is shit all I can write about is having a laugh with the family and eating my meals, and dossing about in the house. so I've had a doss about have had my fill of rice and so after the moshahree has been put up I'm off to bed, GOODNIGHT AND GOD BLESS

DAY FIFTEEN   : Sunday 27 March 1994

LOCATION   : Sylhet   DESTINATION : Around Sylhet
TEAS : 07

WEATHER   : Raining then turned fine

It rained again today but not as many times as yesterday, but just as hard, and I thought I hope the monsoon season wasn't setting in, but it cleared up for quite a while, long enough for me to visit two more houses for teas 7 and 8, and more cakes, I'm getting used to all this attention. Apart from that nothing happened, the lights didn't go out as often as last night either, and they stopped on till bedtime, I'm getting used to turning in 5 minutes early to put up the mosquito net too, it's worth it though, I fell asleep with my arm against the wall and in the morning there were that many bites on my arm I nearly fell back asleep counting them, better than the sheep theory. another day passed and the last two have been pretty dismal, but I'm hoping things, the weather more than anything, is going to get better, I don't know what's on the agenda tomorrow, I think were off to Durgaphasha if the weather improves, so hopefully I'll have something more to write about tomorrow, so all I have to say is a very very GOODNIGHT AND GOD BLESS.

DAY SIXTEEN   : Monday 28 March 1994

LOCATION   : Sylhet   DESTINATION : Durgaphasha
TEAS : 08

WEATHER   : Sunny

Well I hope we've seen the last of the rain, and it's going to stay like it has been today for a bit longer, we came to Durgaphasha the same way as last time, rickshaw, bus, rickshaw, it wasn't any smoother this time, still bumpy as the grand national ride in Blackpool, but the sun has made up for it today, the village they live in is basic chalet style houses bamboo and mud sides and a thatched roof, not your modern thatch, Bangladeshi thatch not as thick and not as stylish but still as effective. When we arrived, that is Abu, me, Bisab and family which consists of Asma, Bisab's wife, who reminded me of a Asian Debbie Harry when I first met her, her two sons kishwar, and Tanvir, and their sister Dilruba, Abu's cousin Nahina and the hired help Shazia. Most of the people remembered me, well it's not often, in fact they never see a white man, so it's not surprising they did, we went through the greeting of salam alikem and all that, then it was did I remember anything they taught me last time, which mostly I did, then it was a walk to the Bazaar, it wasn't very big but I suppose it does its job because it seems to be doing a lot of trade, I still got some stares, but there all friendly ones, one guy there knew Abu from the village before he moved to London, they chatted a while and when Abu was going the guy said make sure he shows me the village, after a cup of tea from the "cafe"(shed) it was a short walk to the next village to visit a few more friends and relatives, more names to remember then it was back to the Bazaar for another cup of tea and a slice of cake, only this time it was in darkness and lit by a couples of lanterns, proper Victorian times, when we'd had the tea and cake we headed back to our village for some tea, eating food tea, this time, we had tea by candlelight as someone had gone to fetch some paraffin for the lanterns, the village has leccy but the storms put a stop to the luxury living for a while, so the village was in darkness apart from the candles, after tea it was more Bengali lessons with the family, there's not a lot you can do in the dark, apart from chat and laugh, and with me learning Bengali there's quite a few of them flying around. Sassie (Abu's auntie) came and told us supper was ready and it must have been the hottest to date, it burnt me bleeding lips off, then I had a few more Bengali lessons to cool them down, more laughs, more cups of tea and then it was off to bed before I piss myself with the laughing and the tea, were stopping a few days this time so it's really back to basics, I never thought I'd be doing something a Tory told me(but I am), no need to put the mossie net up tonight, Abu's cousins do it for us, so I'm going to turn!. . . blow the light out and get into bed so GOODNIGHT AND GOD BLESS

Got to sleep last night with the sounds of the jungle, well it was like camping out. When I rose up this morning had breakfast, went next door and had another one, and all before 9. 00am. Me and Abu had to wait till a bloke had made us a couple of fishing rods, and then went for a spot of fishing, but we caught nowt maybe next time we'll have better luck. We went back to the village and Abu and Bisab carried on to another village and I stayed at Durghaphasha until they came back, after about 2 or 3 hours Abu and Bisab came back and then me and Abu went to the bazaar again and had another cup of tea and a slice a cake, in fact 2 slices I had one on the way out, I think I will be getting stared at on the way home at this rate, I have never had this many people look at me in my life, even if I walked round Penrith stark bollock naked I wouldn't get as many looks, I said to Abu I must be the talk of the village, and he told me when he and Bisab went to the other village this morning they asked them why didn't you bring the Englishman, now that's fame!. Went to Shazia's parents in the next village now that was really basic bamboo structure with woven bamboo sides plastered with mud for the walls sound medieval times, but it was habitable. There were a couple of more being built and all the thatch was all laid out, and despite what I said the other day it is quite thick. had a cup of tea at Shazia's parents house then it was back to our village. the walk back home was in pitch darkness, Me Abu and Mustakin who came with us must have looked like three blind mice walking home, that's if anyone could see us, when we got back to the village even the lanterns seemed like the lights on Broadway, compared to the trip back, all the kids were playing ludo when we arrived so watched them play that for a while until the tea came and the chatting started, then when the game was over more Bengali lessons, more laughs and I am not being modest now but more compliments Stepen Joe, it was easier to say Stephen Joe than explaining that my proper name was Stephen and my nickname was Joe, so it's Stephen Joe besides most of the people in the village and Bangladesh have double barrel names anyway, "Stephen Joe you are a good man" not my words but true, then after the embarrassment it was another cup of tea then I'm off to bed for another nights kip in the jungle

GOODNIGHT GOD BLESS

DAY EIGHTEEN   : Wednesday 30 March 1994

LOCATION   : Durghaphasha   DESTINATION : Sylhet
TEAS : 10

WEATHER   : Sunny

I was up late today 9-15am, this time yesterday I'd had a wash and eaten two brekkies by now, well I am on holiday! didn't do much this morning just packed my stuff in my bag, which wasn't much and waited for Abu to fetch Shazia from her parents in the next village so we could go back to Sylhet, before we set off back we were invited to go to Shunam Gonj by one of the women, so we will go in about a fortnight. Came back the same way as we went and on the way back we counted twenty six bridges with a bump on either end that's fifty two bumps, not to mention all the other bumps along the way home, when we did get home I wished I only used my arse for shitting out of instead of sitting on it, "the pain!", it takes about a hour and a half to get from Durghphasha and we got home around 4 o'clock had something to eat, then a hours kip, the journey must have took it out of me, I was knackered.

After I got up me and Abu had to go to town for some hay fever stuff for Abu and we saw the kid Abu told that I was Ian Botham what a coincidence, as we asked Bisab earlier on if he ever had the same rickshaw driver, he said yes but they turn up around every three months or so, then for my umpteenth rickshaw ride and I've only been in the country for 10 days we went to Bisab friends house for a cup of tea and a plate of noodles, which were very tasty one of the best offering up to now, but he is more affluent than most of the other people that I've visited up to yet, but ten days in there's plenty of time to top the noodles and have something tastier.

Then it was back home in a temple, which is a three wheeled scooter with room in the back for about eight or ten passengers but you don't see one with less than twelve in, plus the luggage and livestock. when we got home I wrote a few postcards that we bought earlier on tonight, then it will be on with the mossie net and my longee and off with the light, back to the mod cons tonight no need to blow out the lights so it's off to bed, don't know what on the agenda tomorrow but who cares!

GOODNIGHT AND GOD BLESS

DAY NINETEEN   : Thursday 31 March 1994

LOCATION   : Sylhet   DESTINATION : Around the house
TEAS : 10

WEATHER   : Sunny

Well today was to hot to do anything apart from a quick game of football with Kishwar and Tanvir, but it was that hot outside that we played in the house, after the game we just dossed around the house lying under the fans to keep cool if there was any space that is, this all happened after breakfast of course, I caught a bit of the sun later on after playing the second leg of the football match outside, had my dinner about 1. 00pm and after that watched all the villagers play their version of hopscotch, back in the house again to cool down. Then later on we had a walk onto the hill to see the view again, had a pipe and that, then went back to the house to do what we do best drink tea, have a chat, have a laugh and eat supper, our turn to put up the mossie net tonight trouble is with this hot weather nothing gets done so leaves my pages empty and me wondering if I'll get to sleep tonight but I'm going to bed and try anyway so its GOODNIGHT AND GOD BLESS

DAY TWENTY   : Friday 1 April 1994

LOCATION   : Sylhet   DESTINATION : Around the house
TEAS : 10

WEATHER   : Raining/fine

Not again I thought woken up by gale force storms once more, but I'm hoping it's not going to last as long as it did last time, fingers crossed. it's been quite fine apart from the odd shower, so let's hope it stays like this for the rest of the day, but it was another day dossing around the house, only 'cos we didn't want to chance the elements against us, so me and the lads had another game of football, indoors again if your wondering, then we all had a look at the damage the storms had done, roofs blown off, huts blown down, and all their belonging strewn all over the vicinity of their homes, it was very sad watching all the villagers repairing their damaged property, yea really sad looking at the aftermath of the storm, it must be hard trying to live your life on limited funds and not reliant on outside help, to be honest it's heart breaking as it's a lot different from seeing it on the TV, I've spoke to some of these people, there not meaningless faces on the box, I can come back to England and live in luxury so to speak, the villagers have no choice. anyway enough of that about 7pm the weather looked settled so we had a ride downtown, I'm getting used to these rickshaws now, well almost. A lot of the stalls were selling fish, veg and street food and had no leccy and were lit up by lanterns, riding down past them all on the rickshaw reminded me of the old black and white films from the twenties, really old fashioned, we got off the rickshaw and had a walk round and bought some julabis to eat, then it was o'driver for another rickshaw ride home, we got in had a cuppa, a bite to eat and hit the sack, not much done again today thanks to the weather, that was it apart from catching Deena out with an April fool gag, which probably was the highlight of a very dismal day, lets hope it's nicer in the morning so it's GOODNIGHT AND GOD BLESS

DAY TWENTY ONE   : Saturday 2 April 1994

LOCATION   : Sylhet   DESTINATION : Around sylhet
TEAS : 10

WEATHER   : Fine

Well it's not been much of a day for me, all I did was climb up one of the hills near the house, but the view was fantastic when we got to the top, green fields, palm trees, and then there were homes scattered round the hills, some stately looking homes and then you had the other end of the spectrum of mud huts dotted around the place too. We passed a place that had had a landslide and left a big gaping chasm between the two pieces of separated land, on the way up and down we noticed all the homes that had been damaged in the storms, when we got back to the house for me it was the squat house and then to bed because my stomach was bad really bad, I felt like I'd been on the piss for three days solid and this was the hangover it's awful, but it's not going to affect my holiday though. The only thing that my illness as affected is my diary's' empty pages.

GOODNIGHT AND GOD BLESS.

DAY TWENTY TWO   : Sunday 3 April 1994

LOCATION   : Sylhet   DESTINATION : Nowhere
TEAS : 10

WEATHER   : Warm and fine

Another day recuperating from my dodgy belly, as you can see from my destination for today I'm not taking any chances this time, being so rough yesterday I forgot to mention me and Abu took Pharul's kids to school, Pharul is Abu's eldest sister, yes school on a Saturday, the funny thing was that it was shut, so Deena, Munna who are Pharul's kids and Dilruba, Asma's daughter, me and Abu came back home, all I did after we got back was see how the kids amuse themselves when there's limited power, TV, toys and you just have the basics to play with. not only do the kids go to school on Saturday but they have a private tutor who comes to the house on Sunday and sometimes through the week as well, I did have a bit of a walk earlier in the afternoon, but that was about the most strenuous thing I did all day. I think its Durgaphasha again tomorrow, am not sure, what I do know is the mossie net is up and my bed is calling, so I had better not let it down had I. Another empty page only I blame myself today

GOODNIGHT AND GOD BLESS

DAY TWENTY THREE   : Monday 4 April 1994

LOCATION   : Sylhet   DESTINATION : Durgaphasha
TEAS : 10

WEATHER   : Sunny

We're in Durgaphasha again today and I am becoming quite a local, I've got past the stage where I notice the conditions that the villagers live in, just the hospitality, friendship and love of the people within the houses I'm visiting, they don't have much but they are happy to share it with you. We arrived about 4o'clock, there was me Abu, Abu's eldest sister Pharul, her three children Deena, Munna and the baby Sazair (now I have introduced everyone in the house that I am staying at) after the hello's and a cup of tea it was off to the bazaar for another cup of tea and a piece of that tasty cake I had last time, sat in the sun a while and then we came back to the village and relaxed in the yard watching the kids enjoying themselves and not stuck in front of a telly playing on a mega- drive then we had a game of Bangladeshi snooker, which not being an expert I only watched, it's nothing like it sounds, no balls and cues, or pockets for that matter, it was quite primitive, counters and a board with the pockets drawn on and sort of shove ha'penny format, but they all enjoyed themselves all the same, who needs technology, the only thing being in Durgaphasha is that with there being no electric it gets dark pretty early and there's nothing to do unless there is a full moon then there's some light otherwise it as me dad would say early to bed early to rise makes a man healthy, wealthy and wise so I'm of to bed.

GOODNIGHT AND GOD BLESS.

DAY TWENTY FOUR   : Tuesday 5 April 1994

LOCATION   : Durgaphasha   DESTINATION : Durgaphasha
TEAS : 10

WEATHER   : Sunny all day.

Apart from the natural jungle noises of the animals, birds and the insects, I got to sleep last night by the sounds of the village neighbours praying or chanting, I'd say they would have been praying for better weather, as the storms over the weekend has caused floods and has washed away a whole years supply of rice for the village, so let's hope none of the people I have met, or those I've yet to meet don't surrender to starvation if nothing can be done, anyway that's what might happen, let me tell you what is happening, not a lot really I've become a right lazy git in the village, because everything is done for you, and when I do manage to do something I need a rest after, cos the sun is red hot beating down on you all day, so I'll leave it to the experts. All I've done today is wash my jeans and t-shirt in the river that runs at the back of the village I'm stopping at, taken a few photos of the surrounding scenery and local landmarks, had a game of snakes and ladders and had something to eat, this is the life. The chanting I mentioned earlier was in fact a Hindu funeral, which they sing and dance for a couple of nights to the sound of drums and then they put the ashes into a claypot and send it off down the river, they follow the urn down the river still singing and dancing till they reach the end of their village then the urn just floats away on its own and that's the end of the ceremony. I love coming to the village, the only thing is it goes dark pretty quick when the leccy off, and there's loads to talk about but nothing to write and the pages don't get filled up, I can't even tell you I'm off to put the mozzie net up, cos its done for me, so all I can say is I'm off to bed so its GOODNIGHT AND GOD BLESS.

DAY TWENTY FIVE   : Wednesday 6 April 1994

LOCATION   : Durgaphasha   DESTINATION : Durgaphasha
TEAS : 10

WEATHER   : One hours rain, then sunny all day

It's been a bit of a sad day today, Shelina, one of the women at the house we stay at, had to go back to her husband's village, so we all gave her a big send off, the good news is, she's back next week, funny thing is me and Abu are coming back next week as well, so I'll be seeing her much sooner than I expected when we were giving her the royal send off. We took some photos of her in her sari and all the trimming that go with it, and she looked very nice too. I started two games of snakes and ladders today, but had to cancel them both, the first was Shelina leaving then the other was called off for dinner. The sun was red hot again today, so you never know I might not come back looking like a milk bottle afterall, apart from a trip to the bazaar to stretch our legs nothing much was done again today. Only in the evening about 6-30pm it goes dark and having no electricity, Tahia one of Abu's auntie's kids must have spent half an hour in all trying to make me jump by creeping up on me, one of the funny things was the windows have wooden shutters and on one of the occasions she did actually make me jump, she darted off and ran into one of the shutters that had swung open and banged her head, and as we all know that laughter is an international language and I started laughing it was that funny even Tahia ending up laughing too, as if to say serves her right, later I watched a game of Bangladeshi snooker, then went to bed as there not a lot to do in the dark, good thing is going to bed early is you GET UP EARLY, at least it bright in the morning so come on bed lets have it. GOODNIGHT AND GOD BLESS

DAY TWENTY SIX   : Thursday 7 April 1994

LOCATION   : Durgaphasha   DESTINATION : Durgaphasha
TEAS : 12

WEATHER   : Sunny all day

I excelled myself today, me and Abu went to the next village to see some more of his relatives and I managed to clock up cups of tea number eleven and twelve to my list. We did this around half five in the afternoon, after me and Abu had spent all day fishing for two fish that we had for supper and they were quite tasty too, I didn't realise how much water I waste back in Penrith when I have a bath, because I have a really good bath using two buckets of water when I'm in Sylhet, and today I only used one bucket and still got hygienically clean, at this rate I'll be having a bath in an egg cup soon. I think were going back home to Sylhet shortly but like I said we are back next week, while we were fishing we took a couple of photos of Nahina who came to show herself dressed up in her sari and all the jewellery and she looked very nice, as they all do when they are dressed up, besides from eating food, fishing and drinking tea that's all I've done today, it's only half ten but it's been dark a few hours now, so I think it's time for bed, again no need to put up the mossie net tonight, so all there is to say is GOODNIGHT AND GOD BLESS

DAY TWENTY SEVEN   : Friday 8 April 1994

LOCATION   : Durgaphasha   DESTINATION : Durgaphasha
TEAS : 12

WEATHER   : Sunny after storms over night.

Another lazy day at Durgaphasha, sounds like a western dun it, I have watched Abu's uncle separate the grain from the grass today and there was none of your fancy machinery or John Deere tractors though!, what he did was lay out all the grain stalks on a square of a wicker like mat in the yard in a circle, then he got three of his cows and walked them round and round on the grain, then after so long he would pick up the grain and re-arrange all of it again back into a circle then he'd start the process again, this was done three or four times before he would pick up all the stalks, which wasn't wasted as it was kept for fodder or bedding for the cows, this left all the grain on the mat which was left out in the sun to dry out ready for preparation, I would of took some photos but there's no film left in my camera, but sassa said there would be more to do later on, so I might get a chance to take some then hopefully, that was the highlight of the day today, were off back to Sylhet tomorrow, but we'll be back in the next couple of weeks, later on I had a few games of ludo and snakes and ladders, when I wasn't lazing around waiting to eat, this is the life forgot to mention the sun, sun, sun, I've got used to seeing it everyday now, it's becoming a good mate up to now, well it's another early night it's about half ten and I can hear my bed calling me again so GOODNIGHT AND GOD BLESS.

DAY TWENTY EIGHT   : Saturday 9 April 1994

LOCATION   : Durgaphasha   DESTINATION : Sylhet
TEAS : 12

WEATHER   : Sunny all day

We said our goodbyes to all the villagers, before we went to the bus stop, hah I say bus stop, where the people decide to stand bus stop, came back the same way we went, and arrived back in Sylhet around 3-30pm and I must have lost a stone travelling back, the heat on the bus was hellish it was like a sauna, the last few days in Durgaphasha for breakfast, I've been having a sort of bun, which is runny dough made from just flour and brown sugar, then each portion is poured into red hot oil until they are brown and not burnt, and these things that I've become addicted to are called handesh, very nice they are too, and let's not forget the humble cup of tea as well!. Pharul and the kids had left earlier on, so me and Abu took Shazia's mum and Shazia's younger brother back to Rynogor, which is a district of Sylhet, the house I'm stopping at is also in Rynogor and my address is 18 Mitali, Rynogor, Sylhet, Bangladesh. after getting in and dumping the bags down, we relaxed for a while to get over the trip from village to town, I did this after saying salam alikem to everyone in the house before trying to get a quick kip, later on after my attempt to get some z's on the board I had tea, which from having fish for most of the meals at Durgaphasha to have meat, beef in fact made a pleasant change. the good thing about Mitali is when permitting the lights are on, so it was a few more Bengali lessons and then I retired to bed, got to put the mossie net up tonight, and it's going up without a doubt tonight, why? we've used the last of the insect repellent so it's going to be fun, I'm expecting to wake up tomorrow with more spots than a set of dominoes, so here goes GOODNIGHT AND GOD BLESS.

DAY TWENTY NINE   : Sunday 10 April 1994

LOCATION   : Sylhet   DESTINATION : Around Sylhet
TEAS : 12

WEATHER   : Sunny

Today me and Abu took Kishwar up the local mountain which we've christened Mount Abu as it hasn't got a name of its own, and I think I might have caught the sun too doing it, you don't think it when you're walking in the sun most of the day but it really knackers you out as well.

When we came back we had something to eat, the house I'm stopping at in Sylhet feels more like a Youth hostel, I only seem to be there when I'm eating and sleeping, but it feels a long way away from one of them, when I am eating there it's 110% family.

After I had my belly full of rice I went to sleep for a couple of hours to get over the walk up that orphan mountain in the blistering desert heat. after the two hours of slumber, I was perked up to some sounds of bhangra music, which I was getting into when the tutor came to teach the kids those extra lessons I mentioned. so it was off to the hill to watch the world go by and take in more sights and scenes of Bangladesh till he had gone. when we got back to the house the tutor had vanished so they must have paid him, so I tried to get another couple of hours kip and I was woken up by Deena holding the baby Abogee, I looked up and got the shock of my life, he'd only gone and had his head shaved, and I mean shaved Kojak style and now he looks a right little cheeky fu. . . sod!, got up and had my daily cup of tea and a Bangladeshi delicacy of a julabi, "nice", then we were called outside to see some lads that had come from Durgaphasa to see Abu, who we met there last week, we had a bit of a chinwag and arranged to meet them tomorrow for some grog, so I'm looking forward to that, now I come to think of it, I haven't had a drink for a month, and I'm not missing it either. I forgot to mention we did take some photos of the views from the orphan mountain though and a couple on the way down of basic village life anyway being back in Sylhet and having the electric on all night it has become a late night

30 minutes past midnight late night, the mossie net is up and I'm getting my head down so it's

GOODNIGHT AND GOD BLESS

DAY THIRTY   : Monday 11 April 1994

LOCATION   : Sylhet   DESTINATION : Around Sylhet
TEAS : 13

WEATHER   : Sunny, but not so hot! but got hotter, wrote to soon.

Since I got back to Sylhet from Durgaphasha I've been getting up quite early around 9am, which is not bad for me, I had my favourite breakfast this morning handesh. washed my jeans, because there's a couple of pigeons flying round the rafters and because there no ceiling they sit on the walls separating the rooms and shit on everything that in the firing line and yes my jeans had been in the firing line, stuck them outside the front door and they were dry for twelve, then it was a quick walk to the hill for a pipe then back to the house, the lads that we were going to meet came round so it was a good excuse for a cup of tea, I feel a bit guilty drinking tea all day when nobody is calling round. then arranged to meet them later, which we did and went to Arif's house for tea number thirteen and I've still got around two months left, but we had to cut the visit short and miss out on the grog, because we went to Chow King Chinese restaurant, yea I know I'm in Bangladesh, or so I thought, anyway we had number 153 and a number 68, I couldn't tell you what Bisab ordered we weren't paying but it was your bog standard Chinese meal barbecue ribs sweet and sour chicken and so on, whatever we had it was a bit of alright and told the owner we would come back when it was me and Abu's turn to pay, and what it costs we wouldn't miss the taka either. When we got back to the house after the meal the time was about half ten at night we had a bit of a chinwag and then I went to bed I thought I was doing alright without the mosquito repellent but this morning my elbow was full of spots like measles so were going to buy some more tomorrow hopefully so its off to bobo's

GOODNIGHT AND GOD BLESS.

DAY THIRTY ONE   : Tuesday 12 April 1994

LOCATION   : Sylhet   DESTINATION : Sylhet
TEAS : 14

WEATHER   : Sunny

What I had planned for today didn't work out, Abu and his sister Pharul took a couple of the kids to Durgaphasha so I thought I'd have a really lazy day, "wrong". I had my breakfast and waited till Abu and the rest had gone, then I relaxed for what I thought was all day, then the kids came in and kept themselves occupied playing with empty cigarette packets, that Bisab had emptied and gave them to play with, were using them as building blocks for nearly a hour when the got distracted when the ice-cream man came past and kishwar went out to buy me a lolly, so when the third interruption came past the B-man, I bought a bunch of bananas for the house, cos the bunches of bananas here can be smaller than you get in the shops and still ripe to eat, but the bunches here can have about thirty odd bananas on your average bunch, costs pence as well. Then me and Ismail, who's only job at the house is to fetch the water from the pump down by the twisted ankle, arse over tit road and fill up the three really big urns at the house for cooking and drinking and went to pick my dry cleaning up, two pairs of jeans, three or four t-shirts shorts and a towel, all came to about two quid English money, not bad I thought, on the way back we called into Ismails' friend Mugbal for my 14th cup of tea for my list, we had a bit of a talk then we headed back home for my tea, I ate my curry and rice, and what I did for dessert I used the same rice I'd had with my curry and mixed it in with one of the bananas that were bought, with a bit of honey poured over, beautiful, banana flavoured rice pudding with honey sorted, Abu and company are not coming back till Wednesday or Thursday so I will try and get my lazy day in then sometime, but now I think it's time for bed, not a bad day to say I had nothing planned so to speak so I'll wish you a GOODNIGHT AND GOD BLESS

DAY THIRTY TWO   : Wednesday 13 April 1994

LOCATION   : Sylhet   DESTINATION : Sylhet
TEAS : 14

WEATHER   : Sunny

I woke up this morning, went to the loo, got back in bed and laid back for five minutes, wrote out the page in the diary for today, had a shave, brushed my teeth, then had my breakfast, waited five minutes for my tea, drank that, relaxed for another five or ten minutes then I realised I had not taken my malaria pills and got a chance to see the clock for the first time this morning and it was twenty past nine, so I reckon I must have been up around eight fifteen, "Pretty good eh! and I forgot to mention I made my bed and wrapped up the mosquito net as well. Later on in the day Asma Abu's youngest sister took another couple of the kids to Durgaphasha too, so that left me, Shazia's mum and Shazia left in the house, so I did what I do best in Bangladesh "relax" and have something to eat and waited for them to come back, which they did around six o'clock, listened to some more Banghra music for a couple of hours or so and then Shazia said that supper was ready so we had supper which was a very tasty bit of chicken may I add, then we had a bit of a chat of what happened at Durgaphasha so after I had heard all the news and goings on and because there's no telly, and to be honest I'm not missing it and I've not seen or read an English newspaper yet and don't intend to either, it is time to hit the sack again, GOODNIGHT AND GOD BLESS.

DAY THIRTY THREE   : Thursday 14 April 1994

LOCATION   : Sylhet   DESTINATION : Sylhet
TEAS : 14

WEATHER   : Sunny

Well today is Abu's birthday and he's twenty one and we're going to celebrate, and I think were going to Chow Kings, this time for an Indian, we didn't end up going for the Indian after all, we went for a walk round the tea gardens of Sylhet and the view was amazing, we took a few photos up there and had a few pipes, something you can't do at Chow kings, and had some coca cola and biscuits, and really let us hair down, the sun was red hot again so after about two and a half hours of walking round the tea gardens we came home had a bit of a rest bite and went out again at night when it was a bit cooler, we only went round the town and stopped for a seek kebab and the old faithful cup of tea, and had another bottle of coke for the way home, I also had one of them julabis things I was talking about there not bad either, but I still prefer the handesh though, Ismail the water boy who came with us bought a pair of jeans not from a shop though it was a guy with a barrow walking round the town, and get this he only tried the jeans on in the street, but over the ones he had on, I couldn't believe it, some experience that was watching him buying jeans Bangladeshi style and don't forget the haggling there was plenty of that too, after buying some stuff for the kids because it happens to be Munnas' birthday today as well, we came home and had a bit of a natter until the rest of the family had finished watching telly, more chat then we had supper and because I don't watch the Bengali programmes there's not a lot to do, only listen to the cassette recorder and as much as I like UB40 there's only so many times you can listen to i'm a creamy donut dum, dum, duumm without going in sane so I think I will go to bed, so here's wishing you a GOODNIGHT AND GOD BLESS.

DAY THIRTY FOUR   : Friday 15 April 1994

LOCATION   : Sylhet   DESTINATION : Sylhet
TEAS : 15

WEATHER   : Sunny again

Who says sunshine make you lazy? well since it's been sunny now for a few days on the trot, all I've have done is get up early and go for a walk and today as been no exception, we had another walk to one of the lads houses that we met the other day and had my fifteenth cup of tea, I'm only counting the cups I've had at other peoples houses, not at home or at the shops these cups don't count. we put the liquid back that we lost walking back with another bottle of coke from the shop and because Friday is the Muslim religious day we had to wait till the shop owner came back from the mosque. later on after we returned home we had some dinner and then we set off to see some fish that's a few hundred years old so they say and if there's any wars or anything like that they disappear till the trouble is over then they come back, and I was glad to say they were there, so that means no wars today anyway. I forgot to say I broke the habit of a lifetime and watched a bit of Tarzan on the TV, actually watching telly makes a change instead of it ruling my life back home in Penrith, I might not even get another one when I get back home, who knows?, I did have a telly at Penrith I just sold everything TV, video and anything else I could sell to have as much money to come here with, and that's about all I did again today, we did take some photos of the fish, they were a lot bigger than I expected, I haven't a clue what were doing in the morning, but what ever we do I'll bet we do it in the sunshine, I'm thirty odd years old and I've never seen so much sunshine on so many days, all I can say is keep shining you beauty, so I will bid you a GOODNIGHT AND GOD BLESS.

DAY THIRTY FIVE   : Saturday 16 April 1994

LOCATION   : Sylhet   DESTINATION : Sylhet
TEAS : 16

WEATHER   : It's Sunny again

Well then d'you know if it wasn't for this diary I wouldn't have a clue what day it was, with the kids going to school on Saturdays, religious days on Fridays and no closing days at the shops on Sunday, no regular telly to go by, the only time I know from the telly is 9 o'clock Wednesday, that's when the A-Team's on, and 11 o'clock Friday, yea you got it that's when Tarzan's on, that's it apart from that the rest are in Bengali, and I'm not that fluent yet!, we had another trip to the tea-gardens today but this time we paced ourselves and it took us around two and a half hours, and I caught the sun again, slowly but surely I'm beginning to acquire a tan, we went to Arif's house and I had tea number sixteen, met a couple of his relatives and went and had another cup of tea with them in a cafe, I tell you since I've been here I've drank some tea and it's not been a month yet, I have worked out on average I'm drinking three cups of tea in different houses a week, I'll tell you something else the tea tastes mainly the same but some of the "houses" are poles apart, from some beautifully designed mansions, that would be deemed unsafe by British standards, but none of the stone building get blown down in the storms, so that says something, to your basic mud huts, the only other thing that is the same is the friendliness of the people living in those homes, when we got back to the house later I was relaxing, as I do best and I was listening to just your everyday sounds of Bangladesh life and was surprised on how many beggars pass by and come to the door, yea beggars at the door, and their hands through the wrought iron doors, we had three the other day, I felt sorry for the ones they gave nothing to, but that's me living in England again, I'd be the same if they came knocking back in Penrith every other day, yea I wouldn't be too happy, the lucky ones that do get something they give them rice or taka, I suppose it all depends on the availability of what they've got. not a lot done again today, but like I said I am on holiday afterall so it's off to bed, the girls have put up the mosharee, that's Bengali for mosquito net, so that means only one thing, means I'm off to bed. GOODNIGHT AND GOD BLESS.

DAY THIRTY SIX   : Sunday 17 April 1994

LOCATION   : Sylhet   DESTINATION : Sylhet
TEAS : 16

WEATHER   : Warm and fine after storms in the morning

I did sod all again today, only because Sunday is my official lazyrestday, Abu and two of his mates went to the tea gardens again, but I never went, I didn't think the weather would stay fine, besides I'll probably see all the bare tea bushes that all my tea has come from so I stayed at home, and just relaxed most of the time Abu was gone, apart from walks onto the hill in between fine patches of weather, and had dinner when they got back, I didn't realise the kids went to school on Sundays as well, I don't know if I've said that before but today I thought they were out playing instead of being in school, they are only at school for three hours so that's why I probably thought they were out enjoying themselves. I think were off to Durgaphasha in the morning so it will be another week of doing fu. . sweet fanny addams, but like I keep saying, "I am on holiday". What me and Abu did this evening was go round all the tailors we could find and see if Abu could get a shirt made in two different colours from the shirt he wanted copied and a pair of jeans that Abu had drawn himself, he was going to buy his own style buttons and design all the pockets and that, after he got that sorted we stopped and had a cuppa, a couple of gulamjams and a piece of cake, then it was o'driver Rynogor and it was a rickshaw ride home, I'm getting used to jumping on them now every time you want to go any where, there cheap and they save the old feet from aching, when we got home we all listened to some more bangra before I went to bed, we still haven't got any mosquito repellent yet, but apart from one night when I fell asleep with my arm against the wall and they attacked me through the net, my arm, from my wrist to my elbow was covered in bites and without exaggeration there must of been over hundred mozzy bites, but they have not been back since though so lets hope they're still stoned and can't be arsed to come back, and they've crossed the white man off the mosquito menu till the end of the holiday. GOODNIGHT AND GOD BLESS.

DAY THIRTY SEVEN   : Monday 18 April 1994

LOCATION   : Sylhet   DESTINATION : Durgaphasha
TEAS : 17

WEATHER   : Warm and fine, later sunny

Got up this morning to lets say a cold looking day, but to be honest it's still
pretty warm, we are going to Durgaphasha today not sure what time yet, so
I packed a bag just in case we go early, by early I mean after breakfast and
before dinner, so I went for a walk on the hill and chilled for a while before I
found out off Abu, who came to the hill to tell me that were going after
dinner today, so that was a cue to have another pipe. Soon after we had
rice we were off to Durgaphasha, only this time we went a different route
and it was different transport, we took the rickshaw to the bus stop, then at
Shunam Gonj we took the launch, which we'd call a sort of barge in Britain,
and the trip wasn't so bad in fact with the sun shining it was quite nice and
peaceful, the scenery kept changing from one paddy field to the next paddy
field to the next paddy field to the. . sorry flashbacks, we arrived at
Durgaphasha around 3-30pm, said all the hellos and salam alikems, put the
bags down then I was whisked off to the next village for my seventeenth
cuppa then as quick as I got there I was on my way back to our village to
pick up Shelina, who's back from her husbands village, then we all went
round to see Daisy, Shelina's friend, where I managed to catch a bit of
English football, but it wasn't this season it was last season when Man
United and Villa were fighting it out till the last couple of games, by the
time I figured out the football were "highlights" of last year it was time for
dinner were having our dinner at Daisy's tonight and because she's a bit
better off than others were having meat, it's not, well for some it might be,
that they can't always afford meat, but why buy food when they can catch
it, so a lot of the curries are fish, so having beef tonight is a nice change, for
dinner we must have had everything, apart from a cup of tea, maybe next
time, then it was back to our village for a few more Bengali lessons from
Mustakin, then into the yard to sit outside under the moonlight for a few
hours, when the moons full it's lighter outside than in the house when the

candles are burning, soon after that I went to the bog while there were still a bit of light, not falling for the middle of the night piss again, it was pitch black with a capital pitch, then it's bedtime for me,

GOODNIGHT AND GOD BLESS.

DAY THIRTY EIGHT   : Tuesday 19 April 1994

LOCATION   : Durgaphasha   DESTINATION : Shunam Gonj
TEAS : 19

WEATHER   : Sunny

We were up, out and had our breakfasts in half a hour this morning to catch the bus for Shunam Gonj, it's about the same distance form Durgaphasha to Shunam Gonj as it is from Sylhet to Durgaphasha, but we travelled a bit of a different way, we got the bus from Durgaphasha to Shunam Gonj and we had to catch a ferry, I say a ferry nothing like P+O, this one held about four buses and took about five minutes, Abu said "we've landed", I didn't even know we had set off, we got into town about 11-30am and had something to eat, chicken curry and a cup of tea, I can't eat anything without a cup of tea nowadays, must be the Englishman coming out in me, then we went and had a shave, the guy that shaved me hardly looked old enough to shave himself never mind me, but having said that though I'm clean shaven and still got both my ears so can't complain, then it was a quick rickshaw ride to get another launch to get to the village we were going to. First stop was to the woman who sometimes stops at Durgaphasha who invited us to stay a few weeks ago, we met a few more relatives of hers', and more of Abu's and then went back for supper and cup of tea eighteen, we had meat again, that's three times on the trot, I'll be coming out in a rash at this rate, after supper me and Abu had to go and sleep at Tofal's house as there was no room at the first house we went to, the bonus for me was we had tea so I got number nineteen on the list, and Tofal's house doesn't have electric either so looks like another early night tonight, I think were back home to Durgaphasha tomorrow so this trip has been short and sweet, so bedtime for me so GOODNIGHT AND GOD BLESS.

DAY THIRTY NINE   : Wednesday 20 April 1994

LOCATION   : Shunam Gonj   DESTINATION : Durgaphasha
TEAS : 20

WEATHER   : Warm & sunny daytime, hailstorm & lightening at night.

I was up the earliest today, I was awake for seven and out of bed for quarter past and I'd not even pissed it, so that's good going for me. We had breakfast at Tofal'shouse and then went back to the village to say our goodbyes to everyone, we were given another breakfast, I could have counted brekkies through my holiday too, with the amount I've had, but this one was only a light one and then we set off for Durgaphasha. We walked back to Shunam Gonj with a couple of stops in between to see more of Abu's relatives and got another cuppa in, that's me in the twenties now, at one of his aunties, it took me and Abu two hours to get to Shunam Gonj to catch the launch back across the river, an o'driver to the bus station, then the dreaded old bone shaker/arse acher of a bus back to Durgaphasha, when we did get back to Durgaphasha would you believe we had to wait for an o'driver, back at the village there was a sort of fair on which the villagers call a milla, me, Abu and some of the kids went and I think I attracted more people than some of the stalls did, so I came back with Abu and then he went back on his own and I stayed at the village and had a few more laughs and games and when Abu got back near or enough supper was ready and when we had eaten we sat outside in the yard watching the lightening, when it started to hailstone, and I am not telling a word of a lie here, they must of been the size of malteazers and they were coming down like bullets onto the corrugated tin roof, this time my ears couldn't stand the noise and I had to cover them with my hands, after the hailstorm, the hailstones were swept away from the doors and some of the kids were having a laugh with the ice as kids do, then we had a snack of mangoes off a tree branch that had been blown down in the storm, and soon after everyone calmed down a bit from all the excitement and slowly filtered off to bed including me, GOODNIGHT AND GOD BLESS.

DAY FORTY   : Thursday 21 April 1994

LOCATION   : Durgaphasha   DESTINATION : Durgaphasha
TEAS : 20

WEATHER   : Warm and breezy

In my diary today's (Thurs) events were written in on Friday morning because I fell asleep Thursday's night. and to make it worse I managed to break my joshmar (glasses) bit of Bengali there for you while I was asleep, just my luck! Anyway lets get back to what happened today, not much again to be honest, just a walk to the bazaar so Abu could get some clothes ironed, jeans, shirts and a few t-shirts, so it was a possibility we might be going back to Sylhet today, because the storm last night ruined more of the villagers rice supplies, so we have to go and tell Pharul, so I packed a bag in case we did, after the bazaar we came back to the village where I watched the women separate the rice from the grass by letting it fall to the ground in a breeze, so that the breeze blew away the grass, and the rice fell to the floor, very simple and very effective. Then it was back to the bazaar to take Shahin to get a lift back to Sylhet, when we came back it was a good laugh, playing football and just having fun in the yard at one stage when Abu and Salma had finished playing badminton one of the really young kids picked up one of the racquets and tried to "serve" one of the kittens by holding it by it's tail and trying in vain to hit the kitten on the head, until one of the bigger kids tried to show him how it "should" be done so I took the kitten off them before it got hurt and put it with it's mother, but it got funnier the mother got up and walked off with the kitten in tow, but the mother walked through the door and the kitten walked on the other side of the door and got trapped between the door and wall, I thought it's not surprising the kitten doesn't know where it's going being held upside down by it's tail by some giant infant trying to send it into space. we did have a bit of good news we don't have to go back to Sylhet today so we stopped for supper, when we'd eaten there were more Bengali lessons by trying to have conversations instead of your basic words and colours and things like that, then like I said earlier I fell asleep.

DAY FORTY ONE   : Friday 22 April 1994

LOCATION   : Durgaphasha   DESTINATION : Durgaphasha
TEAS : 20

WEATHER   : Warm but raining

More bad news for me today, not only did I break my specs last night, cleaning my teeth this morning one of my crowns dropped out, marvellous! I'm just waiting for the third thing to happen, unless my dodgy belly a couple of week ago was it?, hope so!. Like always I didn't do much today apart from get up at seven again, had breakfast again and today I watched all the people of the village harvesting the rice in case any more storms came and ruined more crops, I had dinner and a couple of hours rest to let my meal settle, later on after I had got up I learned to write one to ten in Bengali while Abu visited the paddy fields to see what damage had been done and how much rice they'd lost, when they came back I went to the bazaar with Mustakin for a cup of tea and a julabi, while we were at the bazaar a bloke said "come and look at my mill" and he showed me "his mill", a building the size of a double garage with a machine the size of a small generator in the middle that separated the rice from the grass, I laughed to myself, but in reality it was quicker than the pitch and toss and getting the breeze to do it method used by the women back in the village though, then as it got darkish we went back to the village to have supper which wasn't ready yet so I watched and listened to the kids doing their schoolwork until everyone, and supper was ready, after supper we all sat around the house to go to the bog and that, I've told you about the Durgaphasha version of the black hole of Calcutta going for a piss, so the motto is "do it while the lamps are burning" that's every visit too, sometimes while I'm waiting my turn I think these early nights, some people are just finishing work back in Penrith and Dukinfield, and I'm waiting for bed. so to these people "morning" to the rest GOODNIGHT AND GOD BLESS.

DAY FORTY TWO   : Saturday 23 April 1994

LOCATION   : Durgaphasha   DESTINATION : Durgaphasha
TEAS : 22

WEATHER   : Fine, warm and sunny

Got up pretty early again today, and had my jeans, shirt and socks washed before I had breakfast this morning, after I did have my breakfast I helped to move some of the rice after it had been separated from the grass, it was nothing hard, all the hard work had already been done, it was just a case of moving it into the yard to dry out in the sun, I took some photos of them separating the rice from the grass method with the three cows, I only helped for quarter of a hour or so, then I had to stop, with the sun beating down on you it makes it twice as hard, I don't know how the villagers manage to do it all day, the sun's to hot for me, later on we visited Abu's sassie who is sick, we went and gave our love and said our prayers and left and went and had tea at his brothers house, that tea's my 21st, I should get the key to the tea caddy door today, we came back and did a bit of fishing but drew a blank so we went back to the village and picked up one of Abu's cousins and went to the bazaar for a cup of tea and a piece of cake, which is getting tastier with every piece I have, and on our way back we met a woman who wanted to know and see how Abu's sassie was, so we went back to see her again and would you believe had another tea for the list, making that twenty-two, it doesn't seem two minutes since I was celebrating getting the key to the tea caddy door, how time flies when your having fun, we stopped there quite a while, so by the time we got back it was getting dark and after we had had our supper it was darker still, so it's nearly time for bed, so that means it's a case "just do it while the lamps are still burning" then I'm off to beddy byes, GOODNIGHT AND GOD BLESS.

DAY FORTY THREE   : Sunday 24 April 1994

LOCATION   : Durgaphasha   DESTINATION : Durgaphasha
TEAS : 22

WEATHER   : Raining in the morning, quite hot afterwards

It's a wonder I got to sleep last night, I was sweating like a pig, and I must of smelt like one too, I must of lost a couple of pounds in sweat because of the heat, I did manage some sleep but was back awake about eight, which is very rare back home because of the different style of living, back home, Penrith home two in the morning would be early for me with the nightlife, the listening to the radio and watching TV till the early hours of the morning, after breakfast again I helped out a bit with the grain, like I said nothing to bust my bollocks over, all the hard work had been done, unless they have to separate the rice from the shells by hand, by using a giant pestle and mortar, the pestle operated by two people each have a pestle each and the mortar is huge and the two people in rhythm pound the rice has one brings up the pestle the other comes down avoiding each other in the process, very musical with the sound mixes in with other sounds, such as the praying that goes on five times a day, at first I used to be aware of it happening, but now I'm oblivious to it, I only realise they are praying if they haven't gone to the mosque and they do it at home, then it was off to the bazaar for more tea and cake, we must be making this guy a fortune with the tea and cake we're having, before we went for dinner in Durgaphasha, by someone who invited us who lives in Sylhet, if that makes any sense, it was very nice too, tasty, we had rice, egg, duck and potatoes in a curry sauce and tarka dall, very tasty indeed. then we made our way back to our village and entertained all the residents and guests with my way of learning words that sound the same in Bengali, but in English makes me look a dick, the ones that come to mind are the words for tasty, the word for mosquito and the word for sock, the Bengali words are moshah (mosquito) moshar (tasty) and mozar (sock), so one time I said moshar after eating something meaning tasty, but the word sounded like moshah, and I think they must of thought I guessed I'd just eaten mosquitos for dinner. Anyway today as I told you last week is my lazyrestday so that's all I did today and my bed is calling so I'm not one to let it down, GOODNIGHT AND GOD BLESS.

DAY FORTY FOUR   : Monday 25 April 1994

LOCATION   : Durgaphasha   DESTINATION : Durgaphasha
TEAS : 22

WEATHER   : Sunny

After breakfast today I was at a loose end, so I washed a couple of shirts
and my longhee in the river at the bottom of the garden, I have no excuse
now that the wash-house is shut, I could wait till the tides out I suppose.
The hotter the weather gets the less I manage to do, I did absolutely nowt
until I had my dinner again today, I think picking the rice up off my plate
must have been the most strenuous thing I did all morning, oh I did do a
shift at work, all fifteen minutes worth, moving grain from one of the rooms
to the yard to dry in the sun, then when it had dried in the sun all the
people in the village, including me gathered it up altogether ready for
separation, I wonder if it'll get separated by the cow method, by hand or
will they take it to the local mill at the bazaar, emptied a cart that was full
of straw for fodder for the cows, being pulled by two of the cows that the
straw is for, even the animals work for their keep here, then I went and got
my pay. . . . just kidding, it's terrible trying to get to sleep at night the heat
is unbearable, it's not as if your can strip off or anything because the
mozzies would bleed me dry, so you just have to do your best to keep cool
through the night, so my method is where a long sleeved shirt made of the
thinnest material known to man, and get stoned before I go to bed, and if
the little suckers do manage to get their teeth into me, I'm hoping they will
forget where they got the free drink from. I read a Bengali kids book today
and it was their version of the Solemn Grundy born on budhbar peom?, am
going to try and learn it too?. it will give me something to do in the next few
weeks, few weeks he says. I don't know if anyone has realised yet, because I
haven't thought to tell you but supper at Durgaphasha is always eaten by
lantern or candle, never leccy since I've been here. I just thought I'd tell you
that, I didn't want you to think I had it too easy all the holiday. anyway
these dark nights and long warm days mean only one thing, "early night",
so from me it's GOODNIGHT AND GOD BLESS.

DAY FORTY FIVE   : Tuesday 26 April 1994

LOCATION   : Durgaphasha   DESTINATION : Durgaphasha
TEAS : 22

WEATHER   : Sunny

I couldn't believe myself what time I got up this morning, half past six and definitely not pissed the bed this time, after breakfast we went next door to see the neighbour and guess what he's got malaria, I would have thought that all the local people would be immune to it, we just sat in the yard for a few hours just watching Bangladeshi village life go by, a far cry from back home, I moved more rice from room to yard to dry out, I'll be getting a clock card in a bit, ha ha. . a clock card, ask them for their clockcard they would think it was a clock as thin as card, I don't mind helping out a bit it makes the days a bit shorter, but the sun shining all day makes them seem to stretch out longer though, a bit confusing!, I only help for about a hour or so, otherwise I have a chance of drowning in my own sweat, I can't believe how much sweat I've lost and I'm still here and not flowing down the side of the street with the shit and piss in the gutter, I can see myself I've lost weight but it's not through lack of eating, the food here is not fattening, it's the desert like heat that does it, talking of eating after dinner I had my daily trip to the bazaar for tea and cake, and I'm getting quite a regular there too! came back to the village and gave them another hand to get the rice together and put the straw in the shed, then after that it was off to the river for a bath to get rid of the straw that got down the back of my neck, then it was another doss around the house until supper was ready trying to learn more Bengali, I'm getting there slowly but surely, then there's something else I'm getting used to early nights, but to be fair even I think it's been a long day today, so I'm not going to break a habit of the holiday I'm going to go to bed so GOODNIGHT AND GOD BLESS.

DAY FORTY SIX   : Wednesday 27 April 1994

LOCATION   : Durgaphasha   DESTINATION : Durgaphasha
TEAS : 22

WEATHER   : Sunny, because it's always sunny.

I am getting fed up of writing "got up early this morning" it would be easier for me to write when I got up late, I'm up early every day lately, nothing new being out of bed and dressed for 8am, the only downfall is that, this combined with the hot weather I'm having to get my head down for a couple of hours in the afternoon to recover from exhaustion, dehydration or just your plain laziness, whatever you want to call it I need the rest!. I had my afternoon nap today after Shelina had gone back to her husbands village after a moderate send off compared to last time she was off, I'm not sure when she is coming back to Durgaphasha, but I expect she will visit the village when Abu and me go back home to England. After dinner Affa(Pharul)arrived at the village from Sylhet with Munna and little Abogee, to bring me and Abu some more taka, we only had our bus fare back to Sylhet and would've had to gone back today, now we can stop a few more days. After affa went visiting relatives I was relaxing in the bedroom when believe this a lizard around 3 to 4 inches long, including tail fell on my head, from where who knows?, at first I thought it was Tahia who spends most of her time throwing little stones trying to make me jump or wake me up had thrown something, so I flicked my head Denis Law style to see what had been thrown and this lizard landed on the bed and slithered off, I nearly shit myself after discovering what it was, to be honest had I not been on solid shits I would've followed through, I quickly looked around to make sure none of the kids were playing tricks, and I was alone in the house, now I did shit myself, only kidding, after the reptile drama we had another trip to the bazaar for my usual cup of tea and julabi, with all the tea we've been drinking Abu is no longer a coca cola addict but now addicted to tea, at least you might have all your teeth when your older, they might be brown but they're be yours mate, we came back from the bazaar and all the kids were asleep, which pleased me in a way, because I thought even the youngest of energy still surrenders to the heat, and my afternoon naps now seem normal, because most of the time when we're all sat around talking one or one of the other kids fan me and the rest of the elders, at mealtimes on the really hot sunny days, so I took the chance to keep them cool while chatting to the rest of the family and fanned them till they woke up, fanning them also keeps the flies, midges and mozzies away, when everyone had woken up and returned from wherever, we all had supper talked for a hour then retired to bed for a good nights kip, so I'll bid you a GOODNIGHT AND GOD BLESS.

DAY FORTY SEVEN   : Thursday 28 April 1994

LOCATION   : Durgaphasha   DESTINATION : Durgaphasha
TEAS : 22

WEATHER   : Guess what it's sunneeeeee

I don't know if I've told you yet, but the kids have been on holiday from school for harvesting, and altogether they are off for a month, the funny thing is you see less of them now, than when there in school, I did a spot of fishing today but I still didn't catch anything, it's been hot today and even the older villagers were having a snooze in the afternoon, maybe I've started a craze, I don't know what the order of the day was before I came did I, so I reckon it must be hot, I relaxed in the yard watching the younger ones playing and using the tools they will be working with later on in life, nothing dramatic has happened today, it's so much of a regular thing the praying fives times a day that you forget to mention it, you can also hear the prayers being broadcast over loud speakers from the mosque all over the town, you can even hear the next door neighbours praying, but it doesn't just happen in Durgaphasha it's all over Bangladesh. I wont forget to mention my daily trip to the bazaar, I will miss that because I think we're going back to Sylhet tomorrow, but we'll be back to Durgaphasha, I will try and get my glasses fixed in Sylhet too, my tooth can wait till I get home, I still have more teeth than some of these Bangladeshi's who eat this leaf called paan with crushed beetlenut and this white paste stuff, you get the paan leaf wipe a bit of the white stuff on it put a few crushed beetlenut in the middle and then wrap it all up in a parcel and then eat it, after years and years of eating this your teeth go black then fall out, it gives me the hiccups more times than not, that's all I did today this is the life what, so it's GOODNIGHT AND GOD BLESS.

DAY FORTY EIGHT   : Friday 29 April 1994

LOCATION   : Durgaphasha   DESTINATION : Sylhet
TEAS : 22

WEATHER   : Sunny Durgapasha : Sunny Sylhet

After breakfast and dinner we set off for Sylhet, on the road from the village to the bus stop, there are parts of it which is covered in grain, drying out in the sun and instead of the cows walking on the grain everything else does people, rickshaws, cars, even buses lend a helping wheel, I timed the journey today from getting on the bus to getting off in Sylhet, it took a hour and a half plus the trips from village to bus stop and from bus stop to home which both took quarter of a hour, so it worked out around two hours, when we got home all the kids didn't seem that bothered after the hello's and what have you, I had a bit of a sleep 'cos the trip and the heat really take it out of you, after another dinner at home in Sylhet and a cup of tea after, then I watched a bit of a Bengali film to try and improve my Bengali, then it was a trip down town for another cup of tea and onion bhaji, after we'd eaten we were walking round when we bumped into the lads we know, after a chat and stroll round town we came home for supper, doing things over here are normal to the locals, which back in Britain would get you some dirty looks, I'm talking about eating meals without any cutlery and using your hand, ever since I arrived I've been eating my meals in this way and never once thought to mention it but I'm getting quite good at it, and the other thing that you get funny looks is same sex best mates holding hands, after supper we chatted for a while the family mainly talked I just listened trying to decipher words I knew from the conversation, because we are back in Sylhet we have to put up our own moshahree tonight so it's UP with the net and ON with my longee and INTO bed

GOOD NIGHT AND GOD BLESS.

Well it's been a scorcher today, the temperature was thirty seven point five degrees, but that as to be converted, so until I get back to Britain I haven't a clue how hot it really has been today, but it was hot, so not a lot done again today, after breakfast Arif and Belal came to the house, so we went out and ended up going to visit his sister in hospital in the middle of Sylhet, unfortunately for us she was being seen by the doctor, so we never really got to see her, we did see a couple of convicts in the waiting room escorted by the police, the prisoners have these shackles on their feet and instead of a chain holding them together, it's a metal rod, they have one handcuff on and this is tied with very thick rope to the shackles on their feet, I saw one of them walk in them and you would have thought he was in hospital getting treated for piles, after we had had enough of watching the mincing convicts we came back home for dinner and a rest, this sun really takes it out of you if you walk any distance at all, then after I got up me and Abu had a quick trip down town, if you can have a "quick" trip to town trying to rush down "mount Everest road" without breaking your ankle, for a coke and a biscuit from one of the shops, it's a lot cheaper if you drink the coke in the shop, then you don't have to pay for the bottle, it works out the bottle costs more than the pop itself, we came back to the house and just tried to keep as cool as possible until supper, mostly by lying under one of the fans on one of the beds in one of the rooms, and days like these let me tell you is almost impossible, after we had supper we had a chat until it got a bit cooler, it's still pretty hot around ten at night, still t-shirt weather, well it's time for bed and I hope it's not as hot tomorrow or there will be nothing done again, it's May day tomorrow and I will be thinking of Penrith on Monday when everyone gets arse-holed all through the day, so it's a GOODNIGHT AND GOD BLESS.

DAY FIFTY   : Sunday 1 May 1994

LOCATION   : Sylhet   DESTINATION : Sylhet
TEAS : 22

WEATHER   : Sunny

It's been another scorcher today so all I did was get absolutely "stoned" on the local Bangladeshi "weed" and smoked away my homesickness, my appetite for an English meal, to see another white man, a sip of coffee, half of lager the list goes on, that's all I did with breaks for dinner and supper of course, and the odd trip down town for a tea or coke, it's getting that hot these days I seem to be sweating when I'm sat down when there's no fan on full blast, sometimes I just imagine the house taking off like a helicopter, maybe that's just the weed, I hope it stays sunny just a touch cooler would be nice, the worst thing with this weather is you either lose a couple of pound in bed by wearing clothes to protect you from the mozzies or you just sleep in your longee and chance it, my track record of bites I've been wearing socks and long sleeved shirts, I wear the thinnest I have, like tracing paper but I still sweat buckets most nights and it becomes a second skin by the time I get up, not much done manually again today thanks to this beautiful weather we're having, but mentally it's been fantastic!, going to bed tonight will either be asleep as soon as my head touches the pillow or up all night 'cos I've been stoned all day and half asleep so your guess is as good as mine, now I'm off to put up the moshahree and hop into bed so GOODNIGHT AND GOD BLESS.

DAY FIFTY ONE   : Monday 2 May 1994

LOCATION   : Sylhet   DESTINATION : Sylhet
TEAS : 22

WEATHER   : Hot but not much sun.

Got up this morning around 8o'clock, and after breakfast Abu had a few things to do down town with Bisab, so after they had left for town I switched on the fan and radio and relaxed to listen to bit of English news on the radio, and some news I heard was that of Ayrton Senna who crashed his formula 1 car and died of head injuries, I would have probably been watching that on TV if I had been at home, he was only 34, nearly the same age as me, I'm 34 this November, what a tragedy, that was 10-30am Bangladeshi time! 5-30am English time. After Abu and Bisab came back me and Abu went and had a trip down town to pick up the dry-cleaning and to drop of some material and a shirt, which Abu is having copied in the material he bought, after dropping off the haberdashery we came back to the house and just sat around for half a hour until we went for a curry, it was alright too!, chicken curry(leg)plate of rice a piece plus another in case we want more, gluam jams, paratha and 2 bottles of coke all for 100 taka (£1. 50) tip included, not bad well worth the taka, by the time we got back it was a chat for half a hour, then we went for a stroll onto the hill for a pipe because it was still quite warm for the time of night, after we spent about 40 minutes on the hill we came back to the house and went to bed, it's been a bit of a mixed day today with sad news in the morning rest in peace Ayrton and then a good night, talking of good nights it's time I hit the sack so it's a GOODNIGHT AND GOD BLESS.

DAY FIFTY TWO   : Tuesday 3 May 1994

LOCATION   : Sylhet   DESTINATION : Sylhet
TEAS : 24

WEATHER   : Very hot and SUNNY

Today we had a trip to see the land where Abu and his brothers are going to build their house, it was quite big and the family who are living there until the building starts made us a cup of tea, , and on the way back the teacher who comes to the house to teach the girls, stopped us and we went to his aunties house for another cup of tea, another two for the list, after the tea we came back to the house and rested, we were going to go and visit the tea gardens again but the weather got the better of us, so we didn't bother, it's just as well because Abu and affa Pharul went visiting so I stopped in the house lied on the bed under the fan and went to sleep for a couple of hours, sheer bliss, nice and breezy, no screaming kids for two hours, and perfect silence, when Abu came we all sat outside the front door for a while then me and Abu went to our favourite spot on the hill for a pipe and a chinwag till it was time for supper when supper was over it was time for bed at least the loo is inside the house in Sylhet so the motto can go out of the window tonight, main thing is to remember it in Durgaphasha, these hot days are definitely not filling the pages up.

GOODNIGHT AND GOD BLESS.

DAY FIFTY THREE   : Wednesday 4 May 1994

LOCATION   : Sylhet   DESTINATION : Sylhet
TEAS : 24

WEATHER   : Storms in the night and early morning, then sunny.

Well!. . . what have I done today. . . again not a lot, had a rickshaw ride to a few shops selling cassettes and that, and on the way there I said to Abu lets hope there's a UB40 tape, then I thought to myself we can bin the other one or "lose" it, and the first shop we went into, UB40 tape, Me "how much" Owner"5 taka" Me"2 taka" Owner "3 taka" Me "done" Owner happy Me happy, that was my shopping done for the day, but this what Abu did next would never happen in England, he picked four cassettes bought one of them and owed the taka for the other three, but the shopkeeper never wrote down Abu's name, address, he never asked for ID to say who he was and he let Abu take the cassettes home to play and if he didn't like them could take them back in the morning, trusting or what!, I wouldn't mind if I was trying to find my way back to the shop it would be like looking for a needle in a haystack to me, so lets hope Abu knows where he going in the morning or he likes the tapes or we'll have the local copper after us,.

After we came back to the house it was straight on with the tapes for a hour or so before Abu went and bought Kishwar a bike and the first one on after Kishwar had been on was a Bengali kid, what happened to tails never fails, I hope the tapes are shorter than the films are or I just might have to listen to my UB40 tape in Penrith.

When the bike arrived Kishwar and everyone had a go and the ones that didn't have a go, had a good look at it instead, by this time the day was getting dark so the bike got took in, after the excitement of the new bike had worn off me and Abu went for another curry, only this time I had lamb instead of chicken, it was still ok but I prefer chicken, then we called in at a shop which sell proper ice cream lollies, so we call there when we are flush, then as soon as we got home it was on with another tape to listen to, there's still another to listen to after this, when I'd had enough of listening to the tapes I left Abu to it and went to bed, it's got a bit cooler tonight but I still might have a problem getting to sleep, we'll see. .

GOODNIGHT AND GOD BLESS.

DAY FIFTY FOUR   : Thursday 5 May 1994

LOCATION   : Sylhet   DESTINATION : Sylhet
TEAS : 25

WEATHER   : Storms in the morning again, sunny, storms at night.

On the second of two trips to change one of the tapes we "borrowed" yesterday, Abu spotted somebody he knew from London, Ranu, how he spotted him I'll never know, we were on a rickshaw, Ranu was the middle passenger on a 125 motorbike, we were going in opposite directions, the traffic was like Piccadilly Circus times ten and to top it all Abu had no idea Ranu was in Bangladesh so it's not as if Abu was expecting to see him, when we stopped the rickshaw and met up with Ranu, the strange thing was Ranu was on his way back to meet us, we arranged to meet him later and then left on our different modes of transport for a cup of tea at the house, Ranu and and the other two of Ranu's mates left on the bike and then Ranu came back a couple of hours later and took us back to his house for another tea for the list, after knocking back the tea and knocking up a quarter of a century in teas me and Abu came home from Ranu's so Abu could go and watch an Indian film with Arif and all that lot, so I stopped in the house till he returned, I don't know if there as been any news in England about a hurricane or something in the Bay of Bengal, it said it was heading north from the south, our house is in the north and with the storm we had tonight, I thought it had already arrived, but luckily it passed over within a couple of hours, what made it worse the light and everything went off too!, then when the light came back on we had supper, but the lights went off again before we had time to finish it, but by now I'm used to eating my meals by lantern light or by the light of the flickering candle, after we had finished our supper in the dark, within 5 or 10 minutes the lights came back on so Abu played one of the tapes he swapped at the shop, then I went to bed still listening to the falling rain on the corrugated tin roof, which was still coming down but only in showers, the mozzie net's up, so I'm going to hit the back of it.
GOODNIGHT AND GOD BLESS.

DAY FIFTY FIVE   : Friday 6 May 1994

LOCATION   : Sylhet   DESTINATION : Sylhet
TEAS : 25

WEATHER   : Sunny after storms in the night.

Went down town today and bought a pair of sunglasses, seeing as my normal ones are still knackered, I am going to try and get them fixed just for travelling home in, otherwise who knows where I might end up, I really look the business now though in my shades, got back home after the shopping and had dinner around 2o'clock, then had a walk to our favourite spot on the hill we sat there for a hour or so and then Ranu came and we ended up stopping another two and a half hours just talking before Ranu had to go home again, me and Abu went back to the house and just lazed about waiting till the people that was stopping left the table so we could eat supper, in the meantime there was a bit of a storm again just for about a hour, do you remember I wrote saying that one morning when I got up a bird, the feathered type shit on my clothes, well I got my own back tonight, one of them had either broken its wing or a leg and couldn't fly, so we had it for supper! it was just like chicken, usually me and Abu have a bit of a chinwag after supper but one of the guests was stopping in our room, so after supper we went for a pipe on the hill to get me to sleep tonight with it being so early and that, half ten it is, but I'm gonna try anyway,

GOODNIGHT AND GOD BLESS.

DAY FIFTY SIX   : Saturday 7 May 1994

LOCATION   : Sylhet   DESTINATION : Durgaphasha
TEAS : 25

WEATHER   : Storms in the morning, Durgaphasha sunny and
storms.

We decided to go to Durgaphasha today but we didn't set off till 3 o'clock as we did a bit of shopping in the town first, to get some things for the kids that they had asked Abu to bring next time we went, then it was off to the bus station to get a bus to Durgaphasha, I was still shaking when I got off the bus, that tells you the journey hasn't got any smoother since we last came, to be honest I could come back in twenty years and it would probably be the same bus and the roads would be worst than they are now, I stopped shaking by the time we sat down at the cafe for a cup of tea and a slice of cake before we jumped on a rickshaw and headed towards the village, going past the paddy fields and with the harvesting well under way, all the green fields are slowly disappearing as each field has it's plants picked to dry out, to leave about three feet of water that the rice used to grow in, another thing I noticed was, but it might of been because we came pretty late today, but there was no one drying any rice on the road on the way to the village, but we'll find out tomorrow if they are still doing it.

When we arrived in the village, we said our salam alikums and told sassie how long we were staying and gave the kids their things they asked for, we had only been in about 20 minutes and it started raining it was quite windy and it started thundering and lightning, it was still warm and the sky was this sickly yellowery colour, like it had jaundice, it was very different to what I'd seen before, after the storms had passed and the sky had recovered and was looking the colour it should be we left it in the yard and went in for supper, then as the night mostly goes in Durgaphasha after we've had supper it's a good chinwag, a good laugh and then the dreaded early night as were in the village and there is no leccy, I say dreaded early nights I don't mind these early nights in the village because the morning are quite nice 'cos were in the sticks so to speak compared to Sylhet. no need to put the moshahree tonight the girls do it here, so it's stick to the motto and then I'll be going to bed.

GOODNIGHT AND GOD BLESS.

DAY FIFTY SEVEN   : Sunday 8 May 1994

LOCATION   : Durgaphasha   DESTINATION : Durgaphasha
TEAS : 26

WEATHER   : Sunny and showery

After breakfast this morning we went to the bazaar where I got a shave, then my usual cuppa, a bit of shopping and then back to the village and had a bit of a laze around the house and yard till dinner, after we had eaten our dinner we went for a walk, but we had to cut it really short because it started to piss down with rain, while we were sheltering from the rain Abu's cousins who were coming to visit us weren't so lucky they got caught in it as well, so we all had a chinwag until the rain stopped. which were about 25 minutes later so we all came back home for another cuppa, Mustaphis came back later on with a kite frame, and Abu put some polythene on it, went out to fly it, and it actually flew like a proper kite should, all at a cost of about 20p. after the kite flying we went to visit Shazia's mum, we've been many times to visit her before but today it was the first time we had a cup of tea, so that makes it twenty six and still counting, we popped into a couple of houses to visit a few more people on the way out of the village, we also went to see Abu's sick auntie again and it was pitch black but we managed to get there and back, after that we came back to our village and had supper, but before we had time to finish our meal it started to rain again, a perfect cue to hit the sack because the pitter patter of rain on the corrugated tin roof sends me right off to sleep so GOODNIGHT AND GOD BLESS.

DAY FIFTY EIGHT   : Monday 9 May 1994

LOCATION   : Durgaphasha   DESTINATION : Durgaphasha
TEAS : 26

WEATHER   : Sunny

With getting up early while I'm at Durgaphasha it gives me a chance to do some washing before breakfast, this morning I managed to wash my jeans, my longee and a pair of my grundies, that's not Bengali by the way its northern twang for undies, after breakfast we tried to do some fishing again but this time they weren't biting, we must have sat there for a hour or two before we spotted Tofal, who's house we stopped at in Shunam Gonj, who had come to visit us for the day, he'll probably stop at Mitali tonight and go home sometime tomorrow, me and Abu are going back to mitali on Wednesday I think, but we will be back for Eid, after a cup of tea and dinner and like we always do after rice we relaxed, then a bit later on Abu's sassie asked me to help with some hay so I did and it took me two and a half hours. After that we were going to the bazaar but it was to late so we just went for a walk instead, when the three of us came back home for supper, which was meat, I said to Abu are we having meat cos Tofal here, no were just lucky he joked, and then like most nights after supper it's more chinwagging until everyone is ready for bed and I'm ready for bed now so GOODNIGHT AND GOD BLESS.

DAY FIFTY NINE   : Tuesday 10 May 1994

LOCATION   : Durgaphasha   DESTINATION : Durgaphasha
TEAS : 26

WEATHER   : Sunny

We did another spot of fishing today after breakfast for two hours this time, only this morning Abu had caught one within the first 5 minutes we were there, but it was back to normal after that, not having so much of a tickle for the rest of the time we were there. After the fishing we went back to the village to have some dinner, which by now you will have figured out meals are some sort of curry, fish, beef or chicken, but having said that though every one I've had up to now have all tasted different, then went and visited some more of Abu's relations before I watched him play a game of football, it wasn't a bad match, some decent players in full kit and some great ones playing in longees, I say great they must be trying to play football in, basically skirts. The match ended 3-3, so it wasn't so bad of a scoreline that I'd thought it would be, I was expecting more of a basketball score to be honest. Then after the match we went back to the relatives and had tea, seeing as we didn't have time before the match to have it, spent a couple of hours there before we set off home to our village for some supper, today though I got my daily cup of tea from the bazaar and I say hello to this witch doctor and he said he going to sort out some grog, some "smoke" and he's going to sing some village songs, so I'm looking forward to that, we might be going back to Sylhet shortly, but Eid is in about two weeks, so we will be coming back then, I feel like I'm living with nature because when it goes dark I'm ready for bed and in the morning as soon as it's light I want to get up, I think it's because there not much to do in the dark, and it's going dark so I'm off to bed

GOODNIGHT AND GOD BLESS.

DAY SIXTY   : Wednesday 11 May 1994

LOCATION   : Durgaphasha   DESTINATION : Durgaphasha
TEAS : 26

WEATHER   : Storms before 9am, Sunny and breezy onwards

Reading what I've wrote for the weather today when typing up my diary, today is more like a shipping forecast.

Did much the same today as we did yesterday, did a bit more fishing, and today we caught nothing again. Then we went and watched another game of football, this time they all had kits on, but the conditions weren't that good in parts there was about 6 inches of water, so we only watched the first half then we went with the score 0-0, watching it was like watching a Bangladeshi bi-athon, half a game of football and half of swimming, then like any football match as soon as you go early some team scores and they did and to make it worse it wasn't Durgaphasha that scored either, I'll find out the score later if I think on and tell you. After we came home I watched Abu trying to keep the ball off the ground for more than 20, by the time he'd done that we were ready for supper which I fell asleep soon after for a couple of hours(but listen to this)before I got woke up to go to bed, I was happy to sleep in the yard but they said I couldn't sleep outside 'cos all the mozzies would have had a field day, they did have a point though, I think were off to Sylhet tomorrow so I am going back to sleep now,

GOODNIGHT AND GOD BLESS.

DAY SIXTY ONE   : Thursday 12 May 1994

LOCATION   : Durgaphasha   DESTINATION : Sylhet
TEAS : 26

WEATHER   : Sunny Dugraphasha, sunny until 9pm, raining Sylhet.

We set off for Sylhet at noon, not before breakfast of course, which today was Shingari, Shingari is sort of a miniature cornish pasty only the filling is really spicy, not like the plain ones, it's my second favourite breakfast up to today that is, can easily drop a few places if something tastier come along, nothing was done this morning only pack and I had a shave, and soon after that we said our goodbyes and that and left for Sylhet. Travelling on the rickshaw to catch the bus to Sylhet, we saw another bus which had gone off the road and into the ditch, it was close to the bazaar where I have my daily cuppa, luckily nobody was hurt. Apart from seeing that nothing else exiting happened, when we got to Sylhet we had a curry at a restaurant and that wasn't bad either, two plates of rice, two dishes of chicken curry, two teas and extra rice if we wanted it all for 60 Taka including tip a pound in English coin. When we got back to Mitali we just listened to tapes we had, because there's no music at Durgaphasha and with the rainstorm starting at 9pm we couldn't have a trip down town, there's also a couple of people stopping at Mitali tonight too, so supper was late, so we just listened to a bit more music before going to bed, in Durgaphasha one of the girls usually put up the mosharee, whereas here in Sylhet we have to do it ourselves, anyway I cant get to lazy, can I?.

GOODNIGHT AND GOD BLESS.

DAY SIXTY TWO : Friday 13 May 1994

LOCATION : Sylhet   DESTINATION : Sylhet
TEAS : 26

WEATHER : Another scorcher!

Friday the 13th! not as bad as it sounds, today has been quite remarkable(a bit of David Coleman there!)first of all it's been that hot we've hardly done anything, but what we've done has been eye opening. Me and Abu always sit next to this tree on a hill every time we go for a pipe, it looks down onto a road and then into the hills beyond, and sometimes there's a lot of people that pass, some stop, some look, some stop and look, some always talk to Abu like I'm a photograph, is he English, how long's he staying and so on, but today this old bloke came up to me and shook my hand asked me how I was in Bengali, not knowing if I understood him or not, but I did and I told him I was well, and they touch your feet as a sign of respect, so he bent down to touch my feet and he stumbled, I thought he was drunk, in a country where very few places are permitted to sell alcohol I thought no, but he got up talked to Rana who was with us turned to go and went and stumbled again, he was pissed up, he was an Hindu, so we watched him walk down the hill, with his wife who had been standing behind him watching all this happen, for a minute I thought I was back at home. after that Me, Abu and Rana went for a quick walk for a hour and half at the tea gardens, came back and ended up going to Rana's house in the rickshaw because we spent that much time before trying to get one, that when we did got one we thought we'd keep on it and he'll bring us back, only trouble was, he didn't, so we spent a bit longer looking for another one, in the end we got one and luckily there's a shop that we stop at for these great ice-creams between Rana and Mitali, so we stopped and had an ice-cream, when we arrived home it was pretty late, so supper wasn't long, had supper when it came, listened to some music then went to bed not a bad day considering the date.

GOODNIGHT AND GOD BLESS.

DAY SIXTY THREE   : Saturday 14 May 1994

LOCATION   : Sylhet   DESTINATION : Sylhet
TEAS : 26

WEATHER   : Scorcher! until late on then storms

Today we decided to go shopping, so we made our way to, of all places London mansion. I was after a shirt or something and ended up buying a Ziggy Marley tape, (I bet your thinking thick twat does he not know the difference), I do?, but the next "shirt" I buy had better be a Bob Marley one!. Abu bought a pair of jeans and a couple of t-shirts and haggled with the shopkeeper and got 180 Taka knocked off, on the way home we stopped off at a shop to get some batteries for the boom box. When we got home, we put the stuff down, put the batteries in the boom box and went on to the hill to get stoned and listen to the new tapes, Grass, sunshine and Reggae sheer bliss. After that we went home and Abu tried on his new gear and the jeans were a size to big, so he had to go back and change them, which he did with the help of Ranu and his motor-bike, I stopped at home, I could of gone it's only when there is 4 on the bike you get stopped by the coppers, I'm glad I did stop at home because not long after they went the storms started, which caused the lights to go out, and when Abu got back about a hour later the lights were still out, so we all had supper by lantern(which is nothing new nowadays), then after about 2 hours the lights came back on, so we listened to some music until we called it a night, because I think were going to Jaflon on the Indian border tomorrow so GOODNIGHT AND GOD BLESS.

DAY SIXTY FOUR   : Sunday 15 May 1994

LOCATION   : Sylhet   DESTINATION : Jaflon
TEAS : 26

WEATHER   : Sunny in Sylhet and Jaflon, caught in storms on way
home. Raining Sylhet rest of night.

We got up this morning and if we can hire a van pretty cheaply Jaflon is on,
so while Bisab and his mate went to hire the van, me, Abu, Ranu and Ranu's
mate went on to the hill and waited in the sunshine till they came back, in
the end we set off for Jaflon around midday in a sort of mini bus, including
us four, there was Bisab, Shahed, the driver and "his" mate who comes with
the van. It only took a couple of hours and we arrived in Jaflon around 2
0'clock, there were the four of us plus Shahed that went off on our own,
and Bisab, stopped with the driver and his mate. We had a walk down by
the river and it was a bit rough, so what we did we walked until one of the
long boats moving pebbles from one bank to the other had emptied his
load of pebbles and got a lift across the river, we gave him 10 Taka for a 10
minute trip. let me tell you I have never seen so many pebbles in my life"a
million zillion, the other bank was more sandy than stony so we stopped
there for a while having a laugh. Then we spotted a place to swim, only I
can't swim, even at my age, so I rolled up my jeans and I had a bit of a
paddle and the rest had a swim and we messed around in the river, until we
decided to get a boat back across, which we did after a bit of fell walking
and it only cost us 5 Taka this time. After about half a hour playing on the
other side of the river bank we decided to make our way back to the van.
we got back to the van safely and set off back to Sylhet and apart from
getting caught in what I can only explain as a hurricane on the way home,
the only thing that pissed everyone off, was they wouldn't let us over the
border for some photos, but it was a good day, but for me it gets better
(oh! before I tell you about the good news today I wore my Man Utd shirt
all day) I heard on the radio that Man United beat Chelsea 4-1 in the FA Cup
Final and had already won the league (which I didn't know) but I knew they
got beat by Villa 3-1 in the league cup, so today has been a bit of a
celebration after all I heard it on the Bengali news at ten, which is in

English, we got back about half sixish and just talked about the day with the kids and affas till I heard the news on the radio at around 10-15pm then it was a bit of supper, listen to a bit more music and then went to bed.

What a great day for English football,

MANCHESTER UNITED FA CUP WINNERS 1993/94

MANCHESTER UNITED PREMIERSHIP LEAGUE CHAMPIONS 1993/1994

MANCHESTER UNITED LEAGUE AND CUP DOUBLE WINNERS 1993/94

CHAMPIONS. . . . CHAMPIONS. . . . CHAMPIONS. . . . CHAMPION. . . . CHAMPIONS. . . . CHAMPIONS. . . . CHAMPIONS. . . . CHAMPIONS. . . . CHAMPIONS. . . CHAMPIONS.

GOODNIGHT AND GOD BLESS.

DAY SIXTY FIVE   : Monday 16 May 1994

LOCATION   : Sylhet   DESTINATION : Sylhet
TEAS : 26

WEATHER   : Fair, showery and then storms.

I have done nothing apart from feel ill, besides having no dope and seeing no sunshine I've felt rotten all day, I reckon it must have been the non alcoholic celebration I had when I found out Man Utd had won the double, I had a bar of chocolate last night, it was the first bit of chocy I've had since I came to Bangladesh, and it's only worked as a laxative lets say (you might be eating). I did manage a trip to the hill, and one to the shop but that's about it really! apart from eating supper, nothing else really happened that doesn't happen every night, it's annoying being ill and doing nothing, because it's a waste of paper!

GOODNIGHT AND GOD BLESS.

DAY SIXTY SIX   : Tuesday 17 May 1994

LOCATION   : Sylhet   DESTINATION : Sylhet
TEAS : 26

WEATHER   : Sunny until 3. 30pm then storms and showery.

Not a lot happened again today, caused by the weather, not laziness, (this time anyway) Abu and affa (Pharul) went to book the tickets, well not the tickets the seats for coming home and suss out some shops for souvenirs, but in the end it was a waste of time, he said "there were complications on the booking", mind you that was because Abu wanted to stay for a few week longer and then it pissed down, but we did manage a trip out for some tea and a sweet, which didn't taste as good as it sounded, but it was ok, after that it was back to the house to listen to some more music, I even watched a bit of TV, trying to see if I could recognise any Bengali words I have learned since I've been here. Then we had supper, I've been eating with my hand since I left Penrith and I bet now I could eat a tin of soup, plus most nights we eat by lamplight as well, so I could eat blind-folded too. So that all that's happened today pretty boring really.

GOODNIGHT AND GOD BLESS.

Overleaf of the page in original diary has the ingredients for a Bangladeshi stew I invented

beef cut into cubes, handful lentils per person, 1 small onion per 2 people, new potatoes, salt and chilli to taste

and some green veg called doogie. All the ingredients are what you get in Bangladesh that's reasonably common and cheap.

DAY SIXTY SEVEN   : Wednesday 18 May 1994

LOCATION   : Sylhet   DESTINATION : Sylhet
TEAS : 26

WEATHER   : Sunny

What was another boring day , turned out to be ok, I managed to see live coverage of the European cup final between AC Milan and Barcelona, although it was in black and white I thoroughly enjoyed it, I'm writing on today's page but in fact I was watching the match in the early hours of Thursday at around 12. 15am, I don't know if it's because I see less of the TV over here but it went pretty quick, I wouldn't have thought I'd been watching football for a hour and a half when I think about it, I watched the A-Team earlier on too!, apart from that I sat and listened to my Ziggy Marley tape while Abu sorted out the tickets, when he came back we went on the hill, not only people walk past, a couple of cows passed today on their way to pastures greener I should imagine and there's plenty of that in Bangladesh, I would have been pissed off if it had been raining, but luckily for a change it never did, so a typical day listening to music, getting a tan and eating, although I eat regular every day I've still lost weight, I've got a lot of body toning to do when I get back home, anyway that's all I did today not a lot, now I'm off to put the moshahree up then I'm off to bed GOODNIGHT AND GOD BLESS.

DAY SIXTY EIGHT　　　: Thursday 19 May 1994

LOCATION　　　　: Sylhet　　　DESTINATION : Sylhet
TEAS : 26

WEATHER　　　　: Really hot!

On the hill this morning, on the road we look onto we saw an Elephant, trouble is we never have the camera with us, because it's the first one we've seen since we've been here! went to pick up the tickets and according to Abu we head back to England on June 15, earlier than expected but only five days, so we decided to do a bit of shopping for souvenirs, I spent about 500 Taka and I still have stuff to buy. the shopping took up most of the evening and when we came home Shazia made us supper, it was egg which is mixed with onions and chilli's salt and pepper and cooked like an omelette and everything was on the table, we washed our hands and sat down, we started to dish out the grub and then the leccy went off, so we ended up eating supper by the light of the lantern, the electricity was off for quite a while so we all sat outside till the lights came back on, then it was straight to bed as there is someone staying over tonight, I always turn in early when someone stays, I suppose I'm getting fed up of all the questions now, are you English?, how long you staying in Bangladesh? and so on. that all folks for tonight,

GOODNIGHT AND GOD BLESS.

DAY SIXTY NINE   : Friday 20 May 1994

LOCATION   : Sylhet   DESTINATION : Durgaphasha
TEAS : 26

WEATHER   : Like yesterday, really hot.

Got up and had breakfast and got ready for Durgaphasha, had a bit of a sun-bathe on the hill before dinner, then a couple of hours later we set off for Durgaphasha, I didn't like playing sardines at school, but I found myself playing it on the bus, it was quite full today. We've come to the village for Eid which is on Sunday, where they sacrifice a cow for the village to eat while everyone watches, even I'll be watching if my stomach can handle it, we had something to eat as soon as we arrived and later on we went next door for supper. There was a bit of an argument in the house where we sleep so I went outside to sit under the moonlight till it was time for bed and everything had calmed down, it won't be as boring after dark this visit because we've brought the radio today, apart from killing the cow I'm quite looking forward to Eid on Sunday, so with it being another scorcher I'm off to bed I'm goosed

GOODNIGHT AND GOD BLESS.

DAY SEVENTY   : Saturday 21 May 1994

LOCATION   : Durgaphasha   DESTINATION : Durgaphasha
TEAS : 26

WEATHER   : Sunny and very hot hot hot

With the weather being so hot I didn't do much again today, only try to catch the sun which isn't hard, with it being Eid tomorrow I took my jeans and shirt to be washed at the bazaar, a pair of jeans and t-shirt to be washed and ironed and it'll cost about 20 Taka about 30p, Abu had a shave, and then the daily cup of tea, apart from that trip to the bazaar, we stopped in the village all day preparing for Eid, I don't know whether I am looking forward to what's going to happen to the cow or not now it so close, I'll know tomorrow though, it all begins at 6 in the morning, so I'll have something to eat then I'll probably get my head down for the night, so GOODNIGHT AND GOD BLESS.

Overleaf of the page of the original diary is

my first English meal at my mum and dads' is going to be

1 egg and chips,

2 slices of bread and butter,

1 mug of tea, half pint

followed by whatever sweet they have got that I fancy

then if they have toffees or chocolate.

Also at my mum and dads

make a fat Petes' special (a home-made bong).

DAY SEVENTY ONE　　　: Sunday 22 May 1994

LOCATION　　　　: Durgaphasha　　DESTINATION : Durgaphasha
TEAS : 27

WEATHER　　　　: Sunny and hot, rained at night.

EID MUBARAK

I must of got up this morning about 5-45am, that's early for me! I waited for the water to be warmed this morning before I had a bath, cleaned my teeth had a shave, got changed for Eid and had breakfast, then I looked at the clock and it was only seven O'clock. Abu went to pray, but missed it and I went to the bazaar to buy a pen, which by now made the time around eight when the cow was slaughtered, it wasn't as bad as I thought, but there was a bit I couldn't watch for long, then it was skinned, cut up on banana leaves, weighed by hand and the first beef was in the pot ready for cooking at ten, and had my first taste of beef at eleven, now that's fresh meat and it tasted beautiful really tasty, while it was being cooked the kids were running around with drums, made from the broken necks of these pitchers they carry on their head with water or whatever, and the skin from the stomach of the cow stretched over the neck and tied, and left to dry in the sun, which tightens the skin up. After the meal Abu had to go to the sylhet bus stop, so I stayed in the village and just lazed around all afternoon. When Abu came back we just listened to more music, then it was off to the neighbours house for some handesh and my 27th cup of tea in a different house. I will average that out when my holiday is over, it's funny really, of all the times we've come to Durgaphasha it's the first time this guy has invited us in for tea, most probably cos it's Eid, it's like our Christmas, we invite people round who we wouldn't entertain otherwise, but in this case they don't think like that, it was me thinking in English, after the tea and handesh we went back to the house, waited for a while then we had supper, then later on, when everyone was inside it started raining, so it didn't spoil what turned out to be a good day, so its GOODNIGHT AND GOD BLESS.

DAY SEVENTY TWO   : Monday 23 May 1994

LOCATION   : Durgaphasha   DESTINATION : Durgaphasha
TEAS : 27

WEATHER   : Sunny and hot! ended up raining.

We got up as normal this morning, and went for breakfast, guess what! it was beef, but it doesn't sound as bad as that, we had it with chapatis and I thought oh no! but the chapati was well cooked and I ended up having an extra one, when breakfast was over, me and Abu went visiting, we visited Shazia's mum and had a few photos taken of Shazia's sisters, then it was to another village to Shazia's sister in law, after we had visited a few more people in Shazia's village first for shomoi at Shazia's in laws then we had some handesh, then after about a two hour trip and a full stomach we came back to our village, waiting at the village was Shahin (the last member of the family that we stay at Durgaphasha with) who had brought a bottle of grog, so we went for what seemed miles to this village to Shahin's mate and got stuck into the grog and blow!, I smoked the blow through this pipe thing and it wasn't bad either, not the best buzz from a pipe but good, the two cups of grog were good too, we all finished off the grog and the blow and ended up playing the guitar and them having a sing-song, a few songs later me and Shahin went back to the village for about ten and met Abu on the bridge, so we all went back to next door to have supper it was about half a hour later when the rain started, so the people who were in the house stopped and talked, and the younger ones listened to the music, by the time the rain had stopped and all the people had gone and I got the mozzie net up I must have got to bed around one in the morning, I didn't take much rocking, with the blow, grog a full belly and the rain on the roof, I was asleep before my eyes were shut,

GOODNIGHT AND GOD BLESS.

DAY SEVENTY THREE   : Tuesday 24 May 1994

LOCATION   : Durgaphasha   DESTINATION : Shunam Gonj
TEAS : 28

WEATHER   : Sunny in durgaphasha, showery & sunny in Shunam Gonj.

Up, breakfast and out this morning by 9-15am to catch a bus to Shunam Gonj, we went to the bazaar for a rickshaw, but there wasn't any, so we ended up on the launch, which took 35 minutes, I'm not the best of swimmers but it wouldn't have taken me that long to swim it, travelling on the bus to Shunam Gonj, the walk and another launch ride we arrived at our destination at around one o'clock, at the two houses we visited in the village, we were given shomoi, fatra, biscuits and tea(28), we stayed there for a good two hours, then made our way to Abu's auntie at the houses we visited there, we had khoful, jack fruit, pineapple and a main meal of beef curry and rice, we ended up stopping at Abu's aunties house, and after a walk round the fields off the village we came back and had the curry and desert was a banana, we watched the Bengali news before the three of us me, Abu and Shahin went to where we were sleeping had a bit of a chat and then all had an early night, I needed it too! with all the travelling and the walking, not to mention the heat, so it's GOODNIGHT AND GOD BLESS.

LOCATION   : Shunam Gonj   DESTINATION : Durgaphasha
TEAS : 29

WEATHER   : Raining Shunam Gonj, showery in Durgaphasha.

I was up washed and ready for breakfast for 7-30 this morning, for the biggest breakfast yet, on the table was a slice of eggy bread, then came a plate of handesh, then a plate of shomoi, after we had waded through all that, we had tea number 29 to wash it all down with, then we set off back for Durgaphasha, we got a launch across the river Shumar to see Abu's son-in-law house which is rented by some coppers and was given one of their old berets as a souvenir, the bus trip back didn't seem as long and we were back at Durgaphasha for quarter past twelve, and as soon as we got to the bazaar it started raining, the house we stop at, we've not eaten there for two days, as we had dinner next door again, later I got the girls to warm a bit of water, then had a bath, a shave and cleaned my teeth, you need a bath after travelling and stopping out overnight, after I had a bath I had something to eat and planned to stop in the house, as to let Abu go where he wanted with Shahin, seeing as there not long left of the holiday without them asking him questions about me!, after all that he wasn't out long as he got caught in a shower, so they came back to listen to some music, and it literally rained most of the night so we, me and Shahin managed a game of cards in before supper, after we'd eaten I showed him a card trick, then turned in, to have what might be my last night stopping at Durgaphasha, because we are setting off for Sylhet tomorrow, then we are stopping there for the rest of the holiday, but we'll be back to say goodbye though, but now it's GOODNIGHT AND GOD BLESS.

DAY SEVENTY FIVE   : Thursday 26 May 1994

LOCATION   : Durgaphasha   DESTINATION : Durgaphasha
TEAS : 29

WEATHER   : Warm and humid Durgaphasha, ending in stormy
conditions

I thought we were going to Sylhet today, but after I'd packed my clothes and what have you, Abu went and changed his mind, so we ended up stopping, so apart from being pissed off, cos I hate getting ready for one thing than have to do something else, so I just sat around passing the time the best way I know "relaxing" halfway through the day before I knew we were staying, we visited Abu's aunties to say goodbye, then we got back for dinner then still expecting to go to Sylhet, I just waited for Abu to pack his gear, he packed half his stuff then decided to stay, one Stephen Kellegher pissed off! what a waste of day for me!, so because we decided to stay I got stoned! the only thing to do I thought. We had a quick visit to the next village, which is a Hindu village and then we came back for something to eat, by this time the 12 volt battery we've been using for the radio was brought back, so we ended up smoking blow, listening to music and playing cards with Shahin until it was time for bed! Let's hope we don't waste another day tomorrow deciding what to do, there's not many left now!

GOODNIGHT AND GOD BLESS.

DAY SEVENTY SIX   : Friday 27 May 1994

LOCATION   : Durgaphasha   DESTINATION : Sylhet
TEAS : 29

WEATHER   : Sunny and hot in both places.

Got up this morning not knowing whether or not we were going, so today I just waited till Abu said we were going, then I got ready, for breakfast today was, what's slowly becoming my favourite over handesh, and that's shingari and of course my cup of tea, if there wasn't any tea I think I'd be home by now, after breakfast I had a wash, cleaned my teeth as usual, then had a mad half hour with the kids chasing them round the house playing tick, till I got knackered, then back on the bed and under the fan for a rest, I had something to eat around 11 o'clock, we have actually finished off the beef now, but surprisingly enough the beef got better and broke up in your fingers like a chocolate flake as the week went on. Shahin came back to Sylhet with me and Abu but he's not stopping at Mitali, he'll be stopping elsewhere, when we arrived at the house, both affas were out with the girls, and aborgee Kishwar and Tanvir were left at home with Shazia, we had another dinner which was beef, mitali must have some left, we went on the hill for a hour or so waiting for Shahin, but he never turned up, so the rest of the night was spent listening to music, a quick visit to the shop for some tea, had a bottle of Fanta too, and did it taste good, had a walk round then came back to have another cup of tea and then supper, listened to more music before we all turned in for the night, I think we're going to "another" village tomorrow we'll just have to wait and see, I'm getting fed up of waiting around for other people to decide what to do!, especially this close to the end of the holiday, anyway I'll stop moaning and I'm off to bed to get some kip just in case we do go somewhere tomorrow.

GOODNIGHT AND GOD BLESS.

DAY SEVENTY SEVEN   : Saturday 28 May 1994

LOCATION   : Sylhet   DESTINATIN : Mohammad Pur
TEAS : 31

WEATHER   : Showery and warm in both places today.

I think these last two weeks are going to be a bit hectic, visiting all the people who we have arranged to see before we go home and to say goodbye to them all, that explains why were going to Mohammad Pur today. I was up at 7-30am this morning and had mixed fruit jam on toast, the jam was brought from London by Bisab's sister-in-law, who is going to be stopping a few months or so, I had already met her in London before we came to Bangladesh, but to be honest I don't remember her, as I met that many relatives before I came and probably twice as many since I've been here, so to me it's not surprising I don't, the trip to Mohammad Pur took about three hours travelling, but with waiting for the rain to stop, and the walking here and there the trip took from setting out from Rynogor to setting foot in the house in the village, took six and a half hours, a long day. When we got to the house we went to the lake and had a bath while the food was being prepared, after the bath and rice we had a quick walk round some of the paddy fields before we had to make our way back before the rain started, then for most of the night we spent upstairs, it's the first house we've been to that has had a second floor, with the rain coming down when it feels like it, we ended up just talking until it was time for supper, it might have an upstairs, but there's no electricity, so once again it's a early night, mind you, the early nights are not bad now, as we're up early and the days are longer, make the most of them while we're here, that's what I say, I nearly forgot to mention two more cups of tea, making the running total thirty one, and still two weeks to go I might hit the 40 mark at this rate, so I'm off to bed now

GOODNIGHT AND GOD BLESS.

DAY SEVENTY EIGHT   : Sunday 29 May 1994

LOCATION   : Mohammad Pur

DESTINATION : Sylhet via Durgaphasha
TEAS : 32

WEATHER   : Warm and humid, sunny in the afternoon at all three
villages.

We made an early start today, as we had to visit an old bloke in another village, which wasn't bad 'cos I got another cup of tea for the list(32)after waiting about half a hour we caught the launch to Durgaphasha, by this time the sun had come out and it was very hot, so I got a bit of sun-bathing in and had a sleep at the same time. The launch took around three hours by the time we got to Durgaphasha, we said hello and had something to eat, then I washed my longee and t-shirt before we set off for Sylhet, I also had a look at the progress of my fan, that Abu's auntie is making for me, and it's looking fantastic, I can't wait till it's finished. We were quite lucky on the way back because the rickshaw driver flagged down a bus to take us to Sylhet, there's no bus stops or anything like that, if you see a bus that you want you just stick out your hand and bingo, a bus ride to wherever your going, we dropped off the bags at mitali before it was straight out again for something to eat, with it being such a long day when we got back we just listened to some more music before going to bed, tomorrow I think were going out to do a bit of shopping and try and get my glasses fixed, it's not been so bad not wearing glasses but I don't want to travel home without them, I'd probably end up in Timbuktu!

GOODNIGHT AND GOD BLESS.

DAY SEVENTY NINE   : Monday 30 May 1994

LOCATION   : Sylhet   DESTINATION : Sylhet
TEAS : 32

WEATHER   : Raining but still warm.

I slept in this morning 10-30am when I got up, I had breakfast and then got ready for the days shopping, I bought a few bits and bats, three wooden elephants, a fan, no where near as good as the one Abu's aunties making for me and basically treated me and Abu to what ever we fancied, I bought would you believe a Bob Marley tape, well two in fact, but there the same tape, but it makes no odds to me, as the both of them only cost me 60 taka (£1) so I was well chuffed with that and I might get my glasses mended we'll see, I also bought a couple of longees which I didn't know have to be sewn up, so we went somewhere to get them sewn and while we were waiting for them to be done we went to the barbers, Abu had his hair cut and we both got a shave, the full works shave, hot towel job, head and face massage, even the arms and fingers were massaged, brilliant and the music that was on in the shop was excellent, pity we found it to late in the holiday, but it still made my night, we went home feeling really relaxed, so I didn't toss and turn in bed like I usually do with the heat before I went to sleep. GOODNIGHT AND GOD BLESS.

Overleaf of the page of original diary

Fruits I've eaten in Bangladesh(in order of preference)

1=Pineapple

1=Banana(kola)

3=Lychee

4=Mango(aam)

5=Coconut(narkel)

6=Jack Fruit

7=Koful

8=Jaam(a purple grape like fruit grown in Bangladesh)

9=Bori

DAY EIGHTY   : Tuesday 31 May 1994

LOCATION   : Sylhet   DESTINATION : Sylhet
TEAS : 32

WEATHER   : No sun but warm, from 12am rained all day after that.

Woke up early this morning, so after breakfast I washed a couple of T-Shirts, it's just as well I did do them early as it rained for most of the day, apart from that most of the day was wasted due to the rain, spending the majority of the day in the house, we did manage a couple of walks onto the hill in between showers, now until we go home the weather is going to be rainy and stormy, just about sums up the way I feel at the moment!. As long as we can get in a couple more visits to see if I can top the 40 mark with my cups of tea, and a couple of days at Durgaphasha, so let's hope the weather a bit brighter tomorrow, after supper I called it a night after listening to some music for about half a hour. GOODNIGHT AND GOD BLESS.

Overleaf of the page of the original diary,

Bangladesh foods I have had since I've been here,

1=Shomoi

2=Shingari

3=Handesh

4=Fafra

5=Feta

DAY EIGHTY ONE   : Wednesday 1 June 1994

LOCATION   : Sylhet   DESTINATION : Sylhet
TEAS : 32

WEATHER   : Stormy and raining.

This morning the rain started at 10am and didn't let up until about 3-30pm, so all I did until then was have breakfast, listen to music and feel miserable, I don't like this rain. When it did stop, Abu went to have his photo took with both Affas and all the kids, they asked me but I said have a family picture and I'll have a copy. When they all got back, me and Abu went to visit Abu's uncle, and he gave me some shomoi and that bowl of Shomoi confirmed that it had taken over first place from the handesh, which has been relegated to third place, Shomoi would make a great breakfast in England, it's a bit like ready brek but tastes much better, we also had a cuppa but it didn't count as I have already had one at his house earlier on in the holiday, they wanted us to stay the night, but we couldn't, so arranged it for the 5 June, now we're in June, I think we'll just be visiting people to say our goodbyes before we leave. When we got back to the house, Ranu called and we also arranged to meet him tomorrow, so I think now I'm slowly winding down and looking forward to going home especially now we're in June, so I'm off to bed now, GOODNIGHT AND GOD BLESS.

DAY EIGHTY TWO   : Thursday 2 June 1994

LOCATION   : Sylhet   DESTINATION : Sylhet border
TEAS : 33

WEATHER   : Raining from 7am, showery all day.

I woke up this morning about 6-30am went to the squat house, got back in bed, then the wind started blowing so I knew there was a storm on the way, and I was right!, it started persisting down from 7am, I couldn't sleep through that, so I got up and had a wash, shave and cleaned my teeth all before 8am, by the time the rain had finished it was to late to meet Ranu, so we went to the outskirts of Sylhet to visit two of Abu's relatives, one in a village called Lochyphasha and one in Golab Gonj. The first village, we got the rickshaw to the station, then got the bus, which only took half a hours drive to where we got off, then another quick rickshaw ride and we arrived at the village. Today's curry was the freshest chicken I have ever had, we were talking in the house when I heard this chicken squark, I was going to say to Abu does that mean were having chicken, but I didn't, but we did have the chicken, it was being throttled for dinner, while the chicken was being cooked, we did a bit of fishing, first cast, one fish, second cast second fish but this one came off the hook and fell back in the water, then he never caught another one while we were there and that was about a hour and a half, Shahed's brother caught one, but that was it, we had dinner and then had to shoot off to see the other relative in Golab Gonj, a short walk and rickshaw ride and we arrived at the village, there I had another cup of tea(33) for the list, I nearly forgot to mention in Lochyphasha I had Shomoi, they must have known I was coming!, they persuaded us to stop the night, so after supper which was meat again, this time beef, we went to where we were sleeping, it won't be the best nights sleep, no mozzie net and plenty of mozzies, the weather is a bit cooler now so that will help a bit, so here goes I'm off to bed GOODNIGHT AND GOD BLESS.

DAY EIGHTY THREE   : Friday 3 June 1994

LOCATION   : Golab Gonj   DESTINATION : Sylhet
TEAS : 33

WEATHER   : Showery with storms

After breakfast this morning, which I must say was the first breakfast I haven't liked, we set off for Sylhet, we walked to the bus stop, well to where the people were waiting "bus stop eh" and we timed it well, because we near enough walked straight onto the bus, after the bus ride, a rickshaw ride and a short walk up the track, we arrived at Mitali around noon. At this rate I'll be glad to get home if the weather gets any worse, it's been raining nearly all day, mind you they did say it was the rainy season, and I can believe it too!. The rain has dictated what we've done today, "nothing", I've tried to dry my jeans in between showers, but they are still wet, Ranu called up but we couldn't go to his home because of the rain, so all we've done today basically is eat and kept the kids amused, let's hope tomorrow will be a bit brighter, I would like to feel a bit more cheerful for when I go home, I want everyone to see me happy for the last couple of weeks, the girls have put the mozzie net up tonight so that means I'm going to hit the sack, GOODNIGHT AND GOD BLESS.

DAY EIGHTY FOUR   : Saturday 4 June 1994

LOCATION   : Sylhet   DESTINATION : Sylhet
TEAS : 33

WEATHER   : Raining, showers most of the day.

The rain seems to be starting earlier every day, today it was 6am but it only lasted a couple of hours, when it does stop raining its fine, not sunny but fine. Egg for breakfast today and I loved it!, we went to the bank this morning and we passed an old bloke doing some soldering, so I asked him to fix my glasses, and he did for 10 taka, they are perfect to go home in, we came back, had some dinner, then Ranu came with the photos we took at Jaflon, they are better than we expected though!, Abu went back down town to pick up some pants "he designed", they make anything here, while I just relaxed, there was no kids causing havoc and I was listening to Bob Marley, it was the next best thing to heaven. After Abu had come back arund 7pm, I'd by then had 2 cups of tea, took the mickey out of the girls teacher, who is one of two people we've met that has got on mine and Abu's nerves, but doesn't that happen wherever you go on holiday, so we took it on the chin. I managed to watch at bit of TV. I had seen Abu's bespoke pants earlier in the afternoon, but they didn't have buttons on, they don't look that bad, but I wouldn't wear them, I've dossed around most of the day and having pillow fights with the kids and what a laugh, I threw a pillow at Kishwar and it over balanced him, he fell back over another pillow and bumped his head on the wall, he was about to cry when I burst out laughing so he never bothered and carried on, after the mad half hour we listened to some music until the leccy went off, it was off quite a while too, we went to the shops after eating our supper by lantern light, came back from the shops and fell asleep on the sofa, got woke up for bed about a hour later and the power was still off, it must of been off for over three hours, by this time it was bedtime anyway, so I'll wish you a GOODNIGHT AND GOD BLESS.

DAY EIGHTY FIVE   : Sunday 5 June 1994

LOCATION   : Sylhet   DESTINATION : Sylhet
TEAS : 33

WEATHER   : Not raining! warm with a breeze.

I've had a day on my own today, Abu and Pharul went to Durgaphasha to sacrifice another cow, the reason being that they have a few problems and so on, they kill a cow and then give it to poor parts of the surrounding villages in exchange for the problems to sort themselves out, which doesn't sound that bad, a sort of karma you could say, so today I've done a bit of everything, had a wash and shave, listened to a bit of Bob and bhangra, watched a bit of TV, it is a bit of TV as well because there's only one channel, washed my longee, I was going to take the girls to school, but the weather looked dodgy so they went on their own, they even go to school on Sundays here, it wouldn't go down well in Britain, not with the English kids. Well there is one more Sunday before we set off home, ten days to be exact, in those ten days we have to stay at the place we should have stayed today, but with Abu being in Durgaphasha it was not possible, and besides with so little of the holiday left, I would personally like to spend it with the people I know, like those at Durgaphasha and here at Rynogor, so we'll see what happens, so not a lot done today for the diary that is, today I have to put the net up myself so when I've done that I'm off to bed.

GOODNIGHT AND GOD BLESS.

overleaf of the page of original diary

Things to look for when I get home,

the football scene

is Leicester City up or down?

is Oldham Athletic up or down?

what's happening in the soaps :-

has Ron Dixon done away with "junkie" Jimmy Corkhill?

also corry and Eastenders and other Brookside news.

Who has died that's famous that I will miss.

buy the cassette 16 ska and reggae hits vols 1 and 2, (Woolworths)

Bob Marley's classic soul shakedown party

written at the bottom of the page, I can't wait!

DAY EIGHTY SIX   : Monday 6 June 1994

LOCATION   : Sylhet   DESTINATION : Sylhet
TEAS : 33

WEATHER   : Dry and warm, but no sun am, sunny pm

After breakfast today, which was beef and chapatis and they tasted good too, we went down town to change Abu's "designer pants", they made them a bit tight, so we dropped them off to get altered, had a fanta, picked up a pair of sunglasses Abu got fixed and then went to fetch the dry cleaning, the last bit of dry cleaning we'll ever have done in Bangladesh, but believe it or not, it wasn't ready, so we came home having spent 20 taka and nothing to show for it. We called at Ranu's house on the way back too!, he's coming back to London and he's trying to get the same flight as me and Abu, from Dhaka anyway, that's the main flight. Later on after we had eaten, and I mean later on it was about 4pm before we got our lunch, we went out with Asma and Shlina, who's stopping at Mitali for a few days and will be going to Durgaphasha when me and Abu go, and visited some relations for tea, bad news for me it didn't count for the list, after chatting and the tea we made our way back to Mitali and arrived home around half seven and guess what?, right the lights were out, without such as a nod of the head or the wink of an eye me and Abu went straight onto the hill to "mellow out", that's when Ranu came and told us about the flight and he's got the same flights as me and Abu, so Ranu "mellowed out" for a bit then went home, by this time it was 9-30pm and the lights were still out, so until the lights came on which was about ten past ten, everyone were sat on the front doorstep, talking and having a laugh under the moonlight and stars, when the lights did come on, me and Abu had our supper, then talked a bit longer while we listened to some music, then Asma made a cup of tea before I decided to go to bed so that leaves one thing to say and that's GOODNIGHT AND GOD BLESS.

DAY EIGHTY SEVEN   : Tuesday 7 June 1994

LOCATION   : Sylhet   DESTINATION : Sylhet
TEAS : 33

WEATHER   : Raining and wet.

We had breakfast this morning before the rain, the good thing about that was, we could plan what we were going to do when it stopped!, so we decided to go and pick the dry-cleaning up again, this time it was ready, on the way back we had an ice-cream from the igloo shop, not many of them either until we go home. Little Aborgee has been poorly today, so he's been whinging all day and not his usual self, and seeing him like that has put a dampener on the day, I watched something on TV this afternoon called Captain Planet and its like a Green Party cartoon telling you to look after the earth, not bad really, it's a good idea to get the kids interested into looking after the planet at an early age, I was going to watch the best 50 goals in world cup history but we had guests, so I had to miss them, even after they went it might still have been on, so I put the TV on and it was, but within 5 minutes the power was off again, Abu had gone out to rent a colour TV and video and some films to watch for the night, when Abu got back with the telly and video and some Indian films to watch, but the power was still off, when the power came back on instead of watching the films Abu had brought back they started to watch some home videos, until the power went off again after about 20 minutes, and it was like that all night like Blackpool illuminations without the colours. when the lights came back on for good it was about 10-30pm maybe later, by this time looking forward to watching the films had worn off, so Abu and his sisters watched the films and I went to bed, I would have only fell asleep watching them anyway.

GOODNIGHT AND GOD BLESS.

DAY EIGHTY EIGHT   : Wednesday 8 June 1994

LOCATION   : Sylhet   DESTINATION : Sylhet
TEAS : 33

WEATHER   : Warm and sunny.

My breakfast this morning brought back memories of when handesh was my favourite breakfast, but I must say that the ones cooked at Mitali are the tastiest in Bangladesh, after brekkie we took the telly and video back to the shop, 250 taka per night, it's not bad works out around £4, including the films, before we got to the shop we got stuck in a rickshaw traffic jam, two long lines of rickshaws, with the odd car and van here and there and all the cyclists weaving in and out of the spaces available and to top it all the sun was beginning to shine brighter, Aborgee is a bit better this morning, only Tanver has the fever today, I wonder who will have it tomorrow, I just hope it's not me!, we had dinner after we got back and after letting my dinner settle we went on the hill for a while before going to see Abu's relatives, the ones' we should have stopped at a couple of days ago, and when we got there the power was off so we sat outside on the patio/roof of the house and had a chat until the power returned, when it did we were given tea, biscuits and a plate of pineapple and later on had rice. after another chat and a quick glimpse at the A-team it was time to go home, by the time we got back to the house it was the latest we've ever been out till, past eleven and we were told there had been a shooting, where I believe two people got shot with a shotgun, it could have been worse, it could have been me and Abu. . no it could have been earlier in the holiday and Abu would have been a bit more vigilant for the rest of the holiday then he has been, we sat outside for a while to see if we could find out what was happening, then we came in and had rice, milk and sugar, homemade rice pudding for supper, I usually have that after my curry for my sweet, sometimes with a banana mixed in with it or I round my curry off with a couple of pieces of jack fruit, so with a good supper inside me I'm off to my bed

GOODNIGHT AND GODBLESS.

DAY EIGHTY NINE   : Thursday 9 June 1994

LOCATION   : Sylhet   DESTINATION : Durgaphasha
TEAS : 33

WEATHER   : Warm and sunny then raining.

From now on everyday is our last day in Bangladesh, our last Thursday, our last Friday etc, so I'm going to make the most of it too!. We are going to Durgaphasha today for a few days before we go home, so after breakfast I packed my bag ready to go, getting up at 7am this morning also gave me time to have a shave, a bath and plenty of time to get ready for the trip, Ranu came round with his mate so we went for a walk on the hill and chatted till 12noon, when the rain came down and cut it short, after the storm and Ranu had left Abu had a bath and I had my dinner. When it was time to set off me, Abu and Shilina got the rickshaw down to the bus-stop, and the trips to Durgaphasha never fail to amuse me, a bus load of passengers and the driver pulls into a petrol station to fill up, made me chuckle a bit, also the change I noticed when I got to Durgaphasha was all the rice fields which were lovely different shades of green had been flooded and all you could see was water, now the thing on the road to our village is not rice drying out but fishing nets, by the time we got to the village and said hello to everyone, I had a look at the fan sassie had made me and it is beautiful, a work of art something I'll treasure for ever, we went next door for a quick hello, it was getting on for 8-0'clock by this time and we had walk to the bazaar for a cup of tea, had another chat to everyone there, then back to have supper, when we'd eaten supper we had more conversation with the family, everyone is here apart from Mustakin, but there is plenty of time for him to come back, as soon as the girls had put the mosharee up I went straight to bed, seeing as I've been up since seven this morning.

GOODNIGHT AND GOD BLESS.

DAY NINETY   : Friday 10 June 1994

LOCATION   : Durgaphasha   DESTINATION : Durgaphasha
TEAS : 33

WEATHER   : Warm and sunny, rainstorm afternoon then just warm
after storm.

Today's breakfast was shingari, which is another favourite of mine, so someone must know were going home, Abu went to see his auntie, so I stayed at the house for another mad half hour with the kids until the rain came down and most of them stayed out in the rain, I'm not keen on getting wet so I made a hasty retreat to the house and had some dinner. When I had eaten me and Shahin went to pick Abu up from his aunties, then carried on to the bazaar for tea, cake and I tried a plate of shomoi, it was nice but it wasn't warm and it was a bit watery, not the best I've had since I've been in Bangladesh, when we got back Abu had a bath and went to the mosque, while I relaxed, I'm really getting used to relaxing now, when Abu came back from the mosque we walked passed the football pitch which Abu had played on earlier in the holiday and with the floods it's under 2ft of water, there were people rowing across it to get home, it rained on and off all afternoon, so we borrowed the radio from next door to listen to until the rain finally stopped, which was just about to late to do anything only chat to each other until supper was ready, it's surprising how quick the time passes when there's not many clocks to look at, and in my case no TV to tell the time by, being so near to going home the only way I can tell the time is, when I'm hungry, it's dinner-time and when I'm knackered it's bedtime, so to cut a long story short I'm knackered, GOODNIGHT AND GOD BLESS.

DAY NINETY ONE   : Saturday 11 June 1994

LOCATION   : Durgaphash   DESTINATION : Durgaphasha
TEAS : 33

WEATHER   : Warm and raining.

Today it's goodbye day to everyone we've met or that Abu already knows in the surrounding villages, so we've been doing a lot of walking around today, most of the houses we visited mostly gave us handesh, but no teas, but I'm not bothered you see because there already on my list, the weather has been a bit of a stinker really, I wish it would either rain or stay fine, this showery weather pisses me off because you can't really plan anything, we got 3 or 4 houses in before we made our way back to the house, we took a few photos and talked to everyone who had come to the house to say goodbye, then we had dinner, well it was nearly tea it was 2 o'clock, all the walking and after my dinner inside my belly I went to sleep for a couple of hours. After my nap was over and I'd had a cup of tea we went to visit another of Abu's aunties, to get to his auntie we had to pass the football pitch again it was still underwater and more people rowing backwards and forwards, in fact they were coming from all angles, there is as much chaos on the water as on the roads to be honest. some of the boats were sort of services if you needed to get across you just got one of the boats to take you across, our problems started when we got a boat, all of us couldn't fit in it, so the first boat load went left, which left me, Shilina, Salma, two other relatives and a couple of the neighbours kids, so we went to visit Daisy while we were waiting, I spoke to Daisy's dad most of the time, about Bangladesh, football and the holiday, while we were waiting at Daisy's we had tea and biscuits before going back to catch the boat, but it had gone so we all came home, the other half were still out when we came back so we just sat around chatting and waited for the rest to arrive, then when they did we all chatted mostly about how we got split up and ended up visited different houses, after the long days which I've been having in Durgaphasha, as soon as I had my supper which it being my last one I ate it in the kitchen, sat on a stool about 3" high with my plate resting on the floor, for me it was the perfect way to end my stay at Durgaphasha, I felt like part of the family, not that I haven't felt part of it all the holiday, I have. Then it was into bed for my last nights sleep at Durgaphasha.

GOODNIGHT AND GOD BLESS.

DAY NINETY TWO : Sunday 12 June 1994

LOCATION : Durgaphasha DESTINATION : Sylhet
TEAS : 33

WEATHER : Showery and warm, but raining in my heart.

With it being our last breakfast, which was quite a big one, everyone posed for photos and what have you and I was really surprised what the time was, it was only 7o'clock, I was expecting half eight quarter to nine, after we'd packed and gone to a couple of houses to say goodbye me and Shahin went to the bazaar, I said goodbye to the people I'd met before and had my last cup of tea there, in fact I had 2 cups as there was a heavy rainfall so we had to stay there, it eased up for about half hour after so we chanced coming home, "wrong", we got about 100 yards away from the bazaar and the heavens opened again, so me and Shahin got a bit "wet" absolutely dripping to be honest on the way back, on the football pitch this time there were people fishing, I've heard of goal poachers but this is going to far. We got back to the house and ate, I had my last meal with sassa, sassie and little Nowadge, then soon after set off for Sylhet. We travelled back to Sylhet the same way we came, bus and rickshaw, we got about half way home when it started to rain again, that was me wet through again, I was still damp from the first shower, I'd given most of my clothes away in Durgaphasha so I had nothing to change into, we had another cup of tea while we waited for the rain to stop, about half hour later we arrived at the house, there were no kids to greet us, Tanvir was with me and Abu, Kishwar was with his teacher having a lesson, Deena and Munna were poorly so that left Dilruba to welcome us home, we had a cup of tea and something to eat after we had put our bags down and said our hellos, you can always tell you're in Sylhet when the power goes off you can't do anything, play cards, watch TV or play the radio so we just sat outside the front door as it was brighter outside than inside, we did manage to catch a bit of TV before the power went off though, a kids cartoon and a world cup preview, at least I'll be home for some, if not all the world cup by the time I do get home, we talked about what had happened in Durgaphasha the last few days. Ranu came round so we had a chat with him for about an hour until it was time to go, around 10pm, the only right thing that has gone right today was that about 5 minutes after Ranu left the power came back on, so me and Abu had a bit of supper and watched some TV before I went to bed, leaving Durgaphasha and not coming back in the foreseeable future hasn't hit me yet, I think I will get that feeling when I'm back in Penrith, I've been part of a family one way or another for 3 months, I will be when I get to London at Abu's and when I get to my mum and dads in Dukinfield, only when I get to Penrith will it hit me for sure when I'm back living on my own, I'll probably think I've gone deaf for the first few days I'm home, so that's the first sad day over with the next one will be the 15 June, so before I wet the pages of my diary with my tears I'm off to bed.

GOODNIGHT AND GOD BLESS.

When I get home I won't know what to do getting up early every morning, today it was 6-10am when I went to the hole in the floor, but don't worry I got back in bed for a couple of hours, when it rains there's a trough which forms the porch over the front door which catches all the rain so I spent part of the morning emptying that, I was quite surprised how much water it held, it filled up a 56 gallon drum and quarter filled the second one, it's the hardest work I've done in Sylhet, having plenty of water I did some washing, put it outside and within a hour guess what? they were dry?, not quite it started raining again, I've got a feeling they won't get dried today either.

I watched a bit of TV until Abu got ready to do some last minute shopping, I bought a poster of Marilyn Monroe and the Bob Marley tape again, I don't mind how many copies I have at less than a quid each, we bought a Lisa Stansfield tape, the English tapes are mostly pirate so if there is any space left on the end of the tape they fill it up with other music and on the end of Lisa's tape was a bit of Northern soul, the first I've heard for three months. After we had listened to the tapes we'd bought Shahin came to see us from Durgaphasha so we got some money and went for a curry and like all holidays you find the best places when your leaving good and cheap it was, when we had eaten and found Shahin a room to stay in for the night we got a rickshaw home, there were that many going somewhere else and Abu kept shouting the wrong driver and missing the vacant ones I started shouting "o'driver Rynogor", eventually we got one and came home.

Once again, the power had been off again but by this time the lights were on, before we arrived at the house we stopped off for a bottle of pop, which we got on tick as we had run out of taka, when we did get home I watched a bit of TV before I went to bed, I was going to watch Cameroon v Columbia, but it wasn't on or I missed it, who knows?, tomorrow will be my last full day in Sylhet and then we fly back on Wednesday for home.

GOODNIGHT AND GOD BLESS.

DAY NINETY FOUR   : Tuesday 14 June 1994

LOCATION   : Sylhet   DESTINATION : Sylhet
TEAS : 34

WEATHER   : Sunny, a rainstorm and warm.

After my breakfast this morning it was a case of what I was going to take home and what I was going to give away, when I had finally decided and distributed out the things to their new owners it was nearly time to go and visit more of Abu's relatives, which is not bad as the first time we visited the houses I wasn't given a cup of tea, and today's cup makes 34 so I might hit the 35 mark, nearly my age, in the end but with all afternoon and all night to go I don't think I'll make it, we'll see, I watched a bit of TV when we got back home and question of sport was on, the match score was Bill Beaumont 13 wins, Ian Botham 14 wins, the programme I was watching was the last in the series, going into the last round, the picture board and the score was 23-23, they both got a picture right, then BUMPH on the screen came BBC TRANSMISSION ENDS, what a basket or words to that effect, in between programmes the ones I can't understand I usually look out of the window and today what a laugh I had, two kids had took this coconut casing off a cow that was munching on it and I don't know who was surprised the most, me or the kids because the cow started to chase the kids for the casing until they dropped it, so the cow started to eat the casing again and the kids took it again and sure enough the cow was in pursuit again until they dropped it for a second time, this happened a couple more times and the cow had chased them all over the place so on the last chase the kids decided to jump up to higher ground, about a foot, foot and a half higher and guess what?, the cow duly followed them, the only way they got away was they climbed over the wall that surrounded most of the higher level, I was in stitches me cos the cow ran faster than the kids and the only way to stop the cow catching them was they dropped the casing it was like something off Benny Hill, apart from that it's been a miserable day, being the last day in Bangladesh doesn't help. I stopped in the house all day with it being my last day while Abu went and had a haircut again, quite a few of

Abu's relatives visited to say their goodbyes, which by the time they had all gone, made my last supper later than normal but still only around 11pm, there wasn't more to do after that only go to bed in Sylhet for the last time, I'd already packed what was left of my stuff that I was going to take with me so I'm going to bed not knowing if I was going to sleep tonight or not, but there's no harm in trying is there?.

GOODNIGHT AND GOD BLESS.

DAY NINETY FIVE   : Wednesday 15 June 1994

LOCATION   : Sylhet   DESTINATION : Dhaka
TEAS : 34 Final count.

WEATHER   : Hot with a bit of sun in Sylhet and Dhaka.

Well I did get some sleep last night and I was up pretty early this morning, I was at the shop for 8am and the shopkeeper was still putting stuff outside on show, bought a coke and said my goodbyes to the bloke and came back to the house for my final breakfast at Mitali, chipatis and chicken curry, a fitting finish to basic food made tasty, I might have told you there are over 45, 000 different kinds of rice, now I can believe that, I most probably have had 25, 000 kinds of them altogether, more relations came to say goodbye and we also went next door to say goodbye, the car came at around 12 noon to take us to the airport, we waited at Sylhet airport for about a hour before boarding the plane, after the goodbyes and the thank yous and that me and Abu got on the plane and sat down next to each other and I'm watching all these Bengalis and Asians getting on the plane, not seeing a white man whatsoever, the steward what ever came to me and Abu and shifted me to a seat on my own, now I'm thinking I have to get someone next to me I don't know, I'd only seen Asians up to yet, now I don't know who was watching my back but I'm looking out of the plane window when I heard the noise of someone sitting down next to me so I looked round to see who I had won for the trip to Dhaka and it was only Ranu, the Ranu who had booked his tickets way after me and Abu, so I fell lucky I could communicate with someone on the flight, but my luck soon ran out after we landed at the airport when I got split up from the rest because I was English and had to go through immigration at Dhaka airport.

LOCATION   : Dhaka airport   DESTINATION : Dubai airport

I think I have to wait till 8-30pm or something and the time now is 4-20pm it's going to be a long wait for me being on my own and having no one to talk to to pass the time away. It's 6-00pm now and I am no closer to getting my flight, apart from the one and half hours I've been waiting, in the time I had been waiting I found out the flight is at 8pm and not 8-30pm so at least I don't have to wait that extra half hour, which would seem like another 3, so things might be looking up, I was on the point of screaming with waiting so long when two records came over the tannoy, the first was feeling, which I only had one and the second one was, are you lonesome tonight! with me being the only Englishman in the airport departure lounge I think someone was talking the piss, I just hope Abu and Ranu are enjoying themselves as much as I am, I'll bet, it's been that long now I've changed my shirt and cleaned my teeth to pass the time, any longer and I'll need another shave!, it's 8-05pm now and it looks like I'm going to wait that extra half hour afterall, 8-35pm and I have actually got my boarding pass and now I have to wait till 9-00pm to get through the flight departure gate, better late than never I suppose, now it's 9-42pm and I have seen the rest of the passengers including Abu and Ranu, and they told me to make a complaint after they had heard what had happened to me, because they were all taken on a bus to a hotel in Dhaka living it up, but I bet the complaint was in the bin faster than I got on the plane, to make matters worse the flight was delayed due to someone trying to smuggle a gun through customs, so we finally took off around 1-15am with Dubai our next port of call.

DAY NINETY SIX   : Thursday 16 June 1994

LOCATION   : Dubai airport   DESTINATION : Rome airport

WEATHER   : Warm for the time of morning

We landed at Dubai airport at around 4-00am in the morning their time, I didn't have a clue whether the clocks had gone back, forward or stayed at Bangladeshi time, we were let off to do some duty free shopping, I bought a couple of cassettes for £3-60p for the two, Ranu bought some fags and Abu bought a snooker cue for £18, when we were satisfied with our purchases we got back on the plane next stop Rome.

LOCATION   : Rome airport   DESTINATION : Heathrow airport,

WEATHER   : Hot and sunny.

We landed in Rome about 9am in the morning again their time, so I think there are only one hour in front of us so that makes it 8am in London according to my calculations and we, after a hours wait on the plane are due into London at around 10-45am according to my ticket anyway.

LOCATION   : Heathrow, London   DESTINATION : London

WEATHER   : Hot and sunny.

The plane landed at Heathrow airport at 11-45am by the time we had walked to where we pick the luggage up it was 12noon not before walking behind a member of the reggae group Aswad, but he must have been crying because he didn't turn around. I still haven't yet set foot on English soil, we waited for our luggage, picked it up and went to get our passports stamped and then made our way out of the terminal, when we got out Abu's brother was there with Kowser his son and Ambias' husband, we actually set foot on English soil at about 1pm. It was about one and a half hours drive from the airport to Abu's mums' house where we were met by his mum, Ambia and Janeth, Abu's sister-in-law Sufia was waiting in the kitchen ready to serve us dinner, we had something to eat before we unpacked the bags, after the meal we had a good talk with the family, unpacked all the luggage, even mine as I had plenty of space in my bags and give the kids their presents when they got home from school, later on Abu went and had a lie down and I went and had a hot bath, the first one in three months, not that I couldn't have had one in Bangladesh it was that hot sometimes you didn't need the water hot. After my bath Abu was still asleep so I had a lie down myself and listened to the local news at 6-35pm from upstairs for a bit till Abu woke up, we are going round to see some of his mates tonight, unfortunately, jetlag must have got the better of me or something because the next thing I remember was looking out of the window and it was pitch black, so I went back to sleep and woke up next morning.

DAY NINETY SEVEN   : Friday 17 June 1994

LOCATION   : London   DESTINATION : Dukinfield

WEATHER   : Warm and sunny.

Having had over 12 hours sleep it wasn't surprising I was up before anyone else in the house this morning, I haven't a clue if Abu got up and went round to see his mates or not yet, as we were going to make arrangements for me to go to Euston train station, so I can go to my mum and dads, I'll have to wait till he gets up now cos I fell asleep as well. I waited for Abu to get up and we had a bit of breakfast, I still haven't had a proper English meal yet. I borrowed some money off Abu and set off from the house around noon after saying my goodbyes and thank yous to everyone who was still at the house, I'm glad Abu came with me to Euston station because after the first time on the underground who knows where I would have ended up, we got to Euston at about twenty to one, and the train was due out at one so there was time for a quick wager at Willie Hills before I said my goodbyes to Abu and got on the train for home, I'd not travelled 5 minutes when I spotted a Eddie Stobart wagon, now that made me a bit homesick for Penrith, the train is due in at Manchester Piccadilly at 3-35pm, so I should be at my mum and dads for around 5 o'clock all being well. The train was near enough spot on time, which surprised me with it being BR, the walk from the train station to the bus stop hadn't half changed since the last time I came, I didn't have to wait long for a bus that was going my way, I was on my last leg of my journey to my parents house, I changed buses and got home earlier than expected, mind you I did add on half a hour in case I had to wait for any buses and that. It was 4-15 when I walked through the door at my mums, it would have been 4pm If I had opened it first, I went in the front room and my dads sat in the chair, looks up and shouts into the kitchen to my mum "look who's here", my mum came to the kitchen door looked at me and said "what you doing here?", I love you too mum I thought. . no the look on her face I thought she was going to pass out, all I did till I had my tea, which is what I said I was having, egg and chips and all the trimmings, I told my parents all about the holiday and what I've been up to since I'd moved up to Cumbria, found out who's died, got married or had kids and so on, went to see my sister-in-law Anne and her mum and dad, which I am glad to say are all ok, my brothers eldest is bigger than me now, I was in the house talking to Bill, Anne's dad when my youngest niece came in and didn't know who I was, Have I been away that long I thought?. I must have been still jetlagged has I never went round to see my mate which I usually drop my cases and it's I'm off to Stus before I do anything else, I bought some solid from my mate who I am not at liberty to say who from and got stoned for the first time in England, which made me a bit absent minded when my mum made me laugh, my dad who I must admit is getting a bit senile now and also forgets things, said to me on one of the occasions I'd forgotten something "you're only jealous because yer dad's a bit vague", I had another bath and because it was at my mums felt better than the one yesterday, it's probably the closest thing I'll get to being at home I suppose, after the bath I just listened to the radio in my old bedroom and ended up falling asleep, I'm expected to get a bit tipsy tomorrow celebrating Manchester United historic winning double with my mate Stu, it won't take many anyway having had 3 units in three months, I'll be staggering walking past the pub to Stu's most probably, so I'm off to bed GOODNIGHT AND GOD BLESS.

DAY NINETY EIGHT   : Saturday 18 June 1994

LOCATION   : Dukinfield   DESTINATION : Dukinfield

WEATHER   : Warm and sunny.

I must be back in my local routine again, I was up at 6-05am and for the first time in 97 days I made my own breakfast, a bowl of porridge and egg on toast, a cup of tea not bad to say I made it myself, I went round to Stu's but he was at work, but called home and get the shock of his life, it made him go grey, went out to the pub at dinner time and I must say I was a bit light headed after two and a half pints, Angela, Stu's wife was working at 4pm, so I stuck it out till then. I was due round Stu's later on to watch Ireland v Italy have a few drinks and catch up on all the gossip, unfortunately it must have had more effect on me than I thought the booze because I slept through till 10pm when my mum said she was off to bed, so my second night was a waste of time too, I'm determined not to waste tomorrow night if I can help it.

GOODNIGHT AND GOD BLESS.

DAY NINETY NINE   : Sunday 19 June 1994

LOCATION   : Dukinfield   DESTINATION : Dukinfield

WEATHER   : Warm and fine.

I got up at 4am this morning, so I listened to some Bob Marley before trying to get back to sleep, I got a couple of hours before I got up for the day, I let my mum make my breakfast this morning after all I'm still on holiday, then I watched a bit of breakfast telly before having a bath and shave, before I took Stu his CD player back, it was just like the old times, breakfast at Stu's, then a trip round the pubs we used to go in, then make our way back and end up in our local, The Albion, for a game of pool, I met another of my mates this dinner Kenny, when I came to my mums I walked past where Kenny lived and I thought then it's a wonder Kenny's not been out to see me, I know now why, he's moved, not moved far away though, just down the street, I was supposed to go round tonight but it must of been the booze again, I must have had all of 4 pints today and I still walked home but they still sent me to sleep all night, so I never got to go round, I came home in the afternoon with Kenny had a good chinwag to see what was going on in Duki and arranged to go round later that night, he went home and I went to sleep and woke up on the Monday morning, so I did end up wasting tonight afterall, GOODNIGHT AND GOD BLESS for last night.

DAY ONE HUNDRED   : Monday 20 June 1994

LOCATION   : Dukinfield   DESTINATION : Dukinfield

WEATHER   : Fine.

I am going to be stopping in Duki till the end of the month, so I am going down the dole to see if I can sign on down here before I return to Penrith. Besides going down to the dole to make an appointment for tomorrow I haven't done much really, with all my mates being at work and me having no cash!, so I've just been listening to the radio, reading the papers, watching a bit of TV, eating and being idle, it's a bit like being back in Bangladesh apart from the papers and sunshine. Talking of music I found out my mate John is touring the USA with near enough his old band The Chameleons, they just changed a couple of members of the old band and the name. Read the local advertiser, I didn't know anyone in it but some of the crime is frightening, you always think it's worse where you live, but I'll be glad to get back to Penrith. Since I've been back on English soil I've not even attempted to watch any football, the ones I would watch are Ireland, Nigeria and Cameroon I think there are more entertaining, the rest are to workman like, anyway I am going to listen to some music then go to bed, it's fantastic not having to go to bed dressed and not waking up full of mozzie bites,

GOODNIGHT AND GOD BLESS.

DAY ONE HUNDRED ONE   : Tuesday 21 June 1994

LOCATION   : Dukinfield   DESTINATION : Dukinfield

WEATHER   : Raining all day.

Had something to eat this morning before I set off for my appointment at 9-00am, I was there before the doors opened, I made a fresh claim, which seems a bit much but I suppose that's the rules. Well it's not bad I had nearly a week without it raining but today made up for that, the rain was quite heavy for England, but only a drizzle compared to Bangladesh, the only trouble in England when it rains everyone freezes their balls off, I got back home wet through so I decided to have another bath and get changed into some dry clothes, having all the mod cons, gas, electric and heating, not that you needed the heat in Bangladesh though, I made myself tea, I mean food tea not the drinking type, I read the papers again, from cover to cover and something that I'd missed without realising it, I miss doing the crossword, so I've been doing that most days, keeps the old grey matter on the ball, not only in Bangladesh did the rain rule what I did but it's done it over here too!, I was going to do a bit of visiting but I didn't 'cos of the rain, so I stayed in all night and listened to music until it was time for bed.

GOODNIGHT AND GOD BLESS.

DAY ONE HUNDRED TWO   : Wednesday 22 June 1994

LOCATION   : Dukinfield   DESTINATION : Dukinfield

WEATHER   : Fine.

I am still getting up pretty early nowadays, so I usually make my own breakfast, I hate having no cash even if I had a bit I would have a walk into Ashton or even Stalybridge but because of the cash flow I've just been stopping in listening to music and even that's the radio as the cassette is playing the tapes to fast and when you've listened to the radio for 3 days the same records keep getting played, so more than not you know what records coming next, or within 2 or 3 records, so that tends to become irritating the more you listen, at least it's not pissing down today, all I've done today is basically realised I've given the dole the wrong number of the house my giro's getting set to, so I phoned up to inform them but I have to go down in person, so that's another walk out for tomorrow. Later on in the evening I went round to Stu's and I got the shock of my life this time, my mate John was sat there, he was back from the states, I didn't think I would see him on this visit, so it was a pleasant surprise, after John and his mum had gone home me and Stu went on the canal for a quick spot of fishing, but we didn't catch anything and it was cut short by some bloke talking a load of shit to us, so we packed up and came home, Stu said I thought he was going to get in the car with us, to tell you the truth I thought he was too!, after I got dropped off at my mum and dads it was about 9-45pm, my mum and dad were ready for bed so I watched a bit of TV, but I am not that bothered anymore whether I watch it or not, I must have watched about a hour before I went to bed as well.

GOODNIGHT AND GOD BLESS.

DAY ONE HUNDRED THREE   : Thursday 23 June 1994

LOCATION   : Dukinfield   DESTINATION : Dukinfield

WEATHER   : Warm and fine.

I woke up this morning and was really surprised at the time, 11-00am, that must be the latest I've been up since I left Penrith, so I had my brunch then went to the dole, I sorted the dole out, then with it being pretty warm I took the long way home and had a walk round Duki and I was amazed at all the buildings that have come down and the new ones built in their places, a big cotton mill where my mate lost his chopper bike has been converted into yuppie flats, there's been an ASDA store built where there used to be a factory and a foundry works, I was thinking walking past and looking at the size of the ASDA building and the land it's built on, they must have some turnover to afford that cash. I walked along King Street and saw the Town hall, even that looks like it's getting a face lift, it's a far cry from when I was arse-holed going to the discos there at the age of 15, I also heard a place where I used to go and listen to northern soul is open again, if that's true I will no doubt go to it before I go home, if it is on that is, I came home through the park and not only have my primary school and my secondary school been demolished but where I used to wag school in the summer house in the middle of the park, now that has been knocked down all my history gone!. When I got back it was round to Stu's house to give him the, I didn't know that was gone, when did they knock that down, how long has that been there and so on then said I'd see him Saturday, went home and had my tea, shortly after my brother's lad David came across from his other grandad's, so I ended up beating him at every card game we played, mind you I did cheat a bit, after he went home I decided to watch a world cup match Italy verses Norway, it wasn't that good, the highlight of the game was when the Italian goalie got sent off, otherwise it would have been a crap match, I was going to watch another match after the Italian game but I fell asleep and woke up in the chair around 4am, saw the time and went to bed.
GOODNIGHT GOD BLESS.

DAY ONE HUNDRED FOUR   : Friday 24 June 1994

LOCATION   : Dukinfield   DESTINATION : Dukinfield

WEATHER   : Sunny and warm, then stormy weather

When I got up this morning my mum had already been out to the papershop and got the days papers, so before I did anything I read the Daily Star, after I had finished reading the paper and found out Ireland were playing a world cup match later today I decided there and then I was going to take "time out" to watch it, so all I did until kick-off was I had a bath, cleaned my teeth and had a shave, I've noticed that I seem to be getting a 5'clock shadow more quickly nowadays, when all the personal hygiene was done I listened to the local radio station until the match was on. The Ireland match was ok but might have been a better game if Ireland had scored earlier on, I hope the next game I watch is better Brazil and the Cameroons, I caught up with what's happening on Brookside, Jimmy Corkhill is in the nick, that's all I wanted to know really!. The Brazil match was alright at least there were more than 1 or 2 goals in it, in all the matches I've watched there hasn't been more than 2 goals, I made my supper after the Brazil game and watched a bit more TV while my supper settled then went to bed and listened to the local radio station before I fell asleep, I almost forgot to mention the storm, although it killed a little girl who got struck by lightening which is a tragedy, but now I can say there's worst storms than that abroad, so lets hope they stay abroad eh!, because you can re-build mud huts and building, where as life is more precious, GOD BLESS that little girl.

GOODNIGHT AND GOD BLESS everyone else.

DAY ONE HUNDRED FIVE   : Saturday 25 June 1994

LOCATION   : Dukinfield   DESTINATION : Dukinfield

WEATHER   : Fine and warm.

I fell asleep last night listening to a talk in, well a phone in, to talk about anything from I didn't like the shoes Lady Di was wearing did you?, to I want to go into conglomerates, that kind of show, well this woman came on telling this story about her son being sick on the train and getting fined all because he left his car at home so he wouldn't drink and drive, but she kept going on to something else and when she realised she was straying from the subject kept saying "any rode" and after about 2 or 3 minutes of none stop talking she'd say "are you with me", two great northern expressions, I had to laugh at a few of the other callers too!. After my breakfast this morning I read the papers and picked out some horses to watch on channel 4 racing, I have no money but it doesn't stop me enjoying it, I always crack on I'm loaded and I put a grand on here and a grand on that, good fun!. The best match I've seen up to yet was tonight's match between Argentina and Nigeria, a bit scrappy at first but end to end stuff, there's been a few good matches these last two days and they seem to be getting better. The northern do I mentioned is on tonight I think, but I am skint and won't be going on this occasion, maybe I will call back one weekend and go then, I have also noticed whether it's because the world cups on but there is a lot of repeats on and the rest is shit, if I didn't watch football I don't think I'd watch the TV at all, I'd just listen to music, which is what I've mostly been doing since I got back to England. When I was watching racing earlier on I didn't realise how many big races I'd missed The National, The Derby, The Oaks and probably a few more, mind you it's just as well the way I pick horses anyway!, I am going to make my supper again tonight then I'm off to bed, as my dad would say "early to bed early to rise, who's going to bed" Bless him.

GOODNIGHT AND GOD BLESS.

DAY ONE HUNDRED SIX   : Sunday 26 June 1994

LOCATION   : Dukinfield   DESTINATION : Dukinfield

WEATHER   : Warm and fine.

Since I got up this morning at about 10am I have hardly done anything apart from read the papers and I'd forgotten how much crap they put in them, looked at the racing results and I must have blew at least two grand in fantasy money, I've not actually had a bet at the bookies yet since I've been back, due to the fact that I've been financially embarrassed since I got home and two I haven't fancied owt, when I get some cash and there's a few horses that I think will win I most probably have a bet until then I'll look at the "form", I listened to the radio till dinner, a proper Sunday dinner too!, last week I didn't know whether I was coming or going but I am getting into the swing of things again now, I listened to the radio a bit longer after dinner before having a bath and shave, having a bath and hot water available all the time I'm like a kid with a new toy, by the time I get home to Penrith I'll look like a prune. In the evening I watched a bit of TV before I made my supper and listened to the radio again and decided to go to bed when there was nowt on the telly, so I was in bed for 3pm!. . only joking.

GOODNIGHT AND GOD BLESS.

DAY ONE HUNDRED SEVEN   : Monday 27 June 1994

LOCATION   : Dukinfield   DESTINATION : Dukinfield

WEATHER   : Quite warm and fine.

I'll say one thing since I've been away and today, I have never had the Monday morning blues, I thought I might have done, being back in the system, It's getting hard to fill up the pages nowadays as I only listen to the radio and watch the TV, in fact I mostly watched the telly today. After my dinner I listened to the radio again till tea-time then I settled down to watch the telly, Corry, then made myself a cup of tea before I watched channel 4's repeat of Graham Taylor's Impossible job documentary, I thought I swore a lot, If I had known he swore that much, I would have put in for the manager's job myself!, when I had finished watching that I made myself supper and did the crossword in the sun till it settled, and then went to bed and listened to some more music, my mums leccy bill might be a bit more than usual, as I can't get to sleep, unless I'm really knackered, without music, It helps to sooth the mind after hectic days of life, not that the last three months have been very hectic, when I was a kid I must have been sent to sleep with lullabies.

GOODNIGHT AND GOD BLESS.

DAY ONE HUNDRED EIGHT   : Tuesday 28 June 1994

LOCATION   : Dukinfield   DESTINATION : Ashton-under-lyne.

WEATHER   : Warmest since I came home, beautifully sunny.

I didn't know what to do today until I signed on, when I'm in Penrith I sign in the morning, here in Duki I don't have to until 3pm to 3-30pm in the afternoon, I could have done half a days work by then, after my dinner I set off and took the scenic route through the cemetery to sign on. After I gave the dole my autograph I had a trip to Ashton Market in the town centre and talk about change, I was pleasantly surprised too!, most of it had been pedestrianised with fancy paving stones, most of the shops have had paint jobs and to be honest not much litter considering it's a busy market, I had a coffee in a cafe looking on to the market and watched and listened to all the folk of Ashton, I heard something else that made me laugh today while having my coffee, when someone said "killing himself laughing", I've not heard that in a long time, I bought a couple of records hoping they were northern soul, I met John in Ashton, so I had a walk around town with him for a while before catching a cab home, glad John was paying for the taxi, I got home around 5pm and made myself a cup of tea, I watched the Ireland v Norway match, now Ireland are in the last 16, after the match I went round to Kenny's and basically stopped at his house till around 10pm sitting in the back garden drinking tea and having a good chinwag, came home to watch a bit more football before I made my supper and went to bed, I hope tomorrow is as nice as today has been,

GOODNIGHT AND GOD BLESS.

DAY ONE HUNDRED NINE   : Wednesday 29 June 1994

LOCATION   : Dukinfield   DESTINATION : Dukinfield

WEATHER   : Fine and warm.

I bet my mum and dad had thought I'd gone back to Penrith this morning because I never got up till 11am, so I had my brunch and read the papers, did the crossword or tried to, it was pretty hard today, I'll have another go later on, what I've been doing today is to try and mend a record player, and I did, the only trouble was, there's no speakers, so I took one out of an old telly, it will do to check my lottery records I bought yesterday to see if i was lucky, one is defo northern, a Bellboys record and the other I'm not so sure!, but I'll keep it just in case, later on I watched the big punch up in Coronation Street, what made me laugh when I read about it in the paper you could see everything, but on the telly they were scrapping in the dark, also I watched Brookside, in fact I'll be glad when I'm back in Penrith because I'm getting back to being a couch potato, having been away I realise now there's more to life than being sat in front of a telly, talking of the telly the BBC and ITV are prejudiced just because Ireland are through to the next round, they never showed their matches live only highlights until now, and in one of the matches the best goal of the tournament was scored. Martina Navratilova is through to the semis' at Wimbledon, I hope she wins it's her 10th title and also her last, I reckon it's only right she should win it as in the past 15 years or so has dominated the centre court, "Good luck Martina", after my stint in front of the telly I made, as I always do, my supper and tried to finish off the crossword, even my mum has had a go and she's better than me a the things and failed, so tonight I am going to bed with a couple of cryptic clues on my mind, until tomorrow when I'll find out the answers in tomorrows papers,

GOODNIGHT AND GOD BLESS.

DAY ONE HUNDRED TEN   : Thursday 30 June 1994

LOCATION   : Dukinfield   DESTINATION : ASHTON

WEATHER   : Hot and sunny.

My body clock is somewhat confused!, Tuesday night I went to bed at 11-30pm and got up next morning pretty late around 11am, went to bed last night about half two in the morning and woke up after thinking I'd had 10 or 12 hours kip, wrong it was only 9-15am, so with me thinking I'd had a good sleep I got up, got dressed and went downstairs and found out the proper time and thought sod it I'm not going back to bed and made my breakfast, I went and sat down on the settee after my breakfast and waited for my giro. . . and waited. . . . . and waited, in the end I had to phone up to see what planet it was on, apparently it was my fault, I hadn't filled a form in, so I had to go down to Ashton fill the form in and take it round to the "big house", the social security offices so called named for it's numerous floors it's got, It took me longer to sort that out than it did to walk down to Ashton in the first place, hopefully it will be here tomorrow, so they said anyway!, I was supposed to be going home today after I had cashed my giro, but now I will have to wait till Monday, travelling on the train on a Friday costs an extra tenner! I thought funk that, Abu told me that it was an extra tenner on Fridays when we got back to London when I wanted to come home the next day but I thought he was taking the piss so I would stay in London for a bit longer, there is something going right for me I have discovered a radio station that plays soul music at least I'm not listening to the same tunes all night, I heard tonight that Maradonna was back on the drugs, allegedly, after watching a bit of telly and about a hour and a half of listening to the radio Kenny's brother came round for me to go out for a couple of pints, so we went to what used to be my local The Wheatsheaf Inn and it wasn't a bad night either, when last orders had gone and the landlord had kicked us out, me Kenny and Antony, Kenny's bro went back to their mums had a couple more drinks and had a bit of supper before I came home, on the way home I cut through my neighbours garden because it's a gable end house of my mums block, I was looking up at the leaking drain pipe as I walked to the path and clang I walked straight into a fire guard/makeshift gate to keep the dog in, I nearly broke my kneecaps but I survived the crutches and managed to walk home, as I had already had my supper at Kenny's mums, I just made a cup of chocolate for myself and then went to bed.

GOODNIGHT AND GOD BLESS.

DAY ONE HUNDRED ELEVEN   : Friday 1 July 1994

LOCATION   : Dukinfield   DESTINATION : Dukinfield

WEATHER   : Warm and breezy.

Spent most of the day helping my little nephew Simon to stick flags in a kids book his mum buys for him, then I ended up cutting out posters of Man Utd players so he could stick them on his bedroom wall, by the time I had done that it was near enough time for dinner, so I made my dinner and went upstairs to listen to the radio for a few hours, I was going to watch racing but decided to have a bath instead, by the time I had done that, had a shave and got dressed and listened to the music for a couple of more hours it was tea time, I had a bit of tea in case Kenny came round to have a couple of pints in the pub. Martina's through to the final of Wimbledon, I missed coronation street because I was out but got back in time for Brookside and I got the shock of my life when I saw Terry Sullivan with a full grown tash and beard, I was going to grow one in Bangladesh, get the photos took then shave it off before I got back, but it was well to hot, and I would have probably looked like Fred Flintstone, brown face with a big white chin, after I had watched Brookside I watched an episode of Red Dwarf and I'd seen it before but it must of been one of the best ones they did, also I had another good laugh at men behaving badly, the part that tickled me was they had a trivia contest in the pub with the girls and the first question was in which film did the Swedish beauty Britt Ekland get her kit off and the girls looked at each other disgusted, the second question was if you bought 3 pints of bitter, 2 packets of crisps and a packet of peanuts, how many johnnies can you get from the machine with the change from a tenner, at this point one of the girls said I'm not staying if the questions are all like these, so he asked a serious question and she stayed then the next question he asked was which film did Demi Moore get her kit off, I just burst out laughing and probably missed a few more good one liners, but never mind I found the programme very funny, then I watched something on Maradonna which was also pretty good, by now it was about half ten, so after a belly full of laughs I had a belly full of supper before I went to bed,

GOODNIGHT AND GOD BLESS.

DAY ONE HUNDRED TWELVE   : Saturday 2 July 1994

LOCATION   : Dukinfield   DESTINATION : Dukinfield

WEATHER   : Fine breezy and warm

I would have been getting up in Penrith this morning if the dole hadn't cocked up my giro, but it's all sorted now and I am going home Monday morning now, after breakfast I read the newspapers and picked some horses, I was cracking on again that I had plenty of money, I was going to go out, but the only spare cash I have will only take me out once so I might go out tomorrow dinner instead, besides I like going out Sunday dinner, sort of a tradition when I was living at home, I sat down to watch racing and after the first race I was well in form, first horse lost!, so in between races I listened to the radio and realised Martina was playing the final so I watched that till it was over, hard luck Martina you did your best, no need to ask me how I did, if you can be imaginary bankrupt, then I am, a bad day at the office, after I had watched racing and tennis next it was football on the agenda but while I was waiting for the footie to come on listening to the radio was brill as the local radio station was playing rave music, which was pretty good to say I'm really into Northern soul, when I sat down to watch footie I was hardly out of the chair till I went to bed, football, quiz, classic comedy then more football, when the second match came on my mum and dad went to bed after the first half, so I watched football with the sound down and had the rave back on, I even listened to the radio in bed it was that good tonight if music be the food of love then play on, that's what Shakespeare said innit so who am I to argue I'll play it,

GOODNIGHT AND GOD BLESS.

DAY ONE HUNDRED THIRTEEN : Sunday 3 July 1994

LOCATION   : Dukinfield   DESTINATION : Dukinfield

WEATHER   : Warm and humid.

It's a good job I'm going home tomorrow, I only just fit all the jargon on the top line today, I had a two course breakfast this morning, toast then cereal, the only cereal I get in Penrith is coronation street, when I'd finished my brekkies I read the papers and I'm still discovering news from months ago, I'm referring to Jimmy White he must of got done while I was away, I had a bath got ready to go out and never bothered, everybody's pleased to see me but I just don't seem to belong here, I feel my body here but my mind is elsewhere, so if I had of gone out I don't think I'd been good company so I stopped in and did my packing in the afternoon so I am ready to go home tomorrow, then It'll be a bit of brekkie and the goodbyes and kisses for my mum and dad then on the bus to Manchester and train home, that's the theory anyway, there's a couple of footie matches tonight which I'll be watching, It's not to bad now it's the knock out stages, no one can play for a draw, the first match although Saudi are out they scored a brilliant goal, I hope the next match is just as good, not a bad match the second game plenty of action, five goals and Argentina out "good result", on the radio was rave again so I listened to that again, the only thing that has let me down while I've been at my mum and dads is normally there is a DJ on Piccadilly that really rips into the people who phone in called James Stanage but he's been on holiday since I've been here and to cap it all he starts back on the radio tomorrow night when I'm back in Penrith and won't be able to pick it up, what a basket!, anyway talking of Penrith I'm up early in the morning to catch the bus so I am off to bed now to get some sleep

GOODNIGHT AND GOD BLESS.

DAY ONE HUNDRED FOURTEEN : Monday 4 July 1994

LOCATION   : Dukinfield   DESTINATION : Penrith

WEATHER   : Fine and breezy, warm and raining

This morning I didn't have time to wipe my arse, I got up at 9-15am and by the time my mum got back from the papershop it was half nine and she had phoned the train times, there was a train at 11-25am from Manchester, but the bus to manny was 10 past 10, so I had a quick wash and shave, two bites of toast and that was only so I didn't take my malaria pill on an empty stomach enough tea to swill them down with and then finish my last bit of packing, said goodbye to my mum and dad and gave them both a kiss and went to catch the bus, while I've been at home I asked Kenny whatever happened to an ex girlfriend of his Jane and he told me the crack and that he hardly ever sees her nowadays, cos she was a really good laugh, and to my amazement she only got on the bus a couple of stops after me so we had a good chat before she had to get off, small world eh!, I arrived in Manchester around 10-50 bought my ticket walked onto the platform where the train was arriving at and only had to wait 20 minutes or so, I bought a coffee and then boarded the train when it stopped on the platform, it took about 2 hours to get to Penrith and I got there about 1-40 in the afternoon and went to Cumbria Training Company to pick up my keys from my landlady and had a good chinwag with everyone I knew, I needed a rest after carrying my bags down there, I set off from CTC for home at about quarter to three and got home at, well to be honest I don't know exactly I had been in a while when it gave the time on the radio as 3-50pm, the only thing that's different from when I went was the garden is overgrown, apart from that I haven't noticed anything different yet, all I am doing tonight is watching football at Billy's who asked me when I was at CTC so here endeth the journey.

A journey and experience of a lifetime.

The journey might be over but the day isn't, I did go round to Billy's then went to Cagney's to see Abu, who I had thought had arrived in Penrith a fortnight ago, but he had phoned up to say he was ill and be back in when he's better so he wasn't there so I stopped and chatted to the lads at the restaurant about the trip and that and the strangest thing happened, after about half a hour Abu came back to the restaurant with Ranu who we met in Bangladesh and a couple of other mates I met in London, what spooked me was when I left Abu's house in London nothing was planned between us to arrive back on the same day but we did spooky.

PHOTOGRAPHS

If you've read the book and wonder why there are no photos, as I mention taking loads while on holiday, unfortunately, in the twenty odd years I had my diary before getting it in print, the negatives of about 100+ pictures have got lost in transit. A shame as it would have been more realistic seeing the conditions alongside my descriptions of what I saw, and taking my word for it.

Stephen Kellegher
2016

Printed in Great Britain
by Amazon